Heart of Heaven, Heart of Earth
and Other Mayan Folktales

HEART OF HEAVEN,

JAMES D. SEXTON AND
IGNACIO BIZARRO UJPÁN

HEART OF EARTH AND OTHER MAYAN FOLKTALES

SMITHSONIAN INSTITUTION PRESS
Washington and London

PRODUCTION EDITOR: Robert A. Poarch
DESIGNER: Janice Wheeler

Library of Congress Cataloging-in-Publication Data

Heart of heaven, heart of earth and other Mayan folktales /
    [compiled by] James D. Sexton and Ignacio Bizarro Ujpán.
        p.   cm.
    Includes bibliographical references.
    ISBN 1-56098-894-0 (cloth : alk. paper). — ISBN 1-56098-770-7
(paper : alk. paper)
        1. Tzutuhil Indians—Folklore. 2. Cakchikel Indians—Folklore.
    3. Tales—Guatemala—Atitlán, Lake. I. Sexton, James D.
    II. Bizarro Ujpán, Ignacio.
    F1465.2.T9H43   1999
    398.2'089'974152—cd21   98-30616

British Library Cataloguing-in-Publication Data available

Manufactured in the United States of America
05 04 03 02 01 00 99   5 4 3 2 1

⊖ The paper used in this publication meets the minimum requirements of the American National Standard for Information Sciences—Permanence of Paper for Printed Library Materials ANSI Z39.48-1984.

The glyphs on the cover, title page, and accompanying the chapter titles are reproduced from Sylvanus Griswold Morley, "An Introduction to the Study of the Maya Hieroglyphs," Smithsonian Institution Bureau of American Ethnology Bulletin 57 (1915). On the cover is an inscription from Stela F (East Side), Quiriguá, Guatemala.

Contents

Preface   *Heart of Heaven, Heart of Earth* is the result of the collaboration between myself, an anthropologist, and Ignacio Bizarro Ujpán, a Tzutuhil Maya Indian who lives in San José la Laguna, which is located on the shores of Lake Atitlán, Guatemala. Ignacio has been working with me for the past twenty-eight years, and this is our fifth book. It contains thirty-three previously unpublished tales. Ignacio is the original storyteller of twenty of these tales; the other thirteen were recently told to him by friends and relatives, both men and women, some living in other towns, both Tzutuhil and Cakchiquel. At the end of each tale I indicate whether the story came from one of these individuals or from Ignacio. Most of these tales are ancient ones that have been repeated in Ignacio's community in various forms for decades, but some of them were invented (rather than simply retold) by Ignacio. When that is the case, I so indicate in the notes, since he was careful to say so himself.

My role has been to translate and edit these tales. Some of them I taped and translated while in the field with Ignacio, who answered any queries I had. Other tales Ignacio wrote and mailed to me, and I translated them at my home office. Any questions that arose during my translation were answered by Ignacio either over the phone or during my visits to Guatemala.

I have written an introduction that provides more detail on how this book emerged from my experiences in Guatemala and that places the tales in their cultural context. My notes also provide further discussion on particular topics. At the end of the book, I have included a glossary designed to aid the reader with definitions of Indian and Spanish words and local expressions.

James D. Sexton

Acknowledgments I should like to acknowledge the help of my research assistants—David Ortiz, Victoria Spencer, Mauricio Rebolledo, Lorenzo Sotelo, and Charles Wright—in translating and editing portions of this book. I should also like to thank James Tate for producing the two maps. In addition, I wish to thank my wife, Marilyn, for reading the manuscript and giving me valuable suggestions. Special thanks go to my son, Randy, for his careful reading and valuable suggestions for improving the narrative flow. Edward Hood, a professor of Spanish at Northern Arizona University, kindly gave me feedback on Guatemalan proverbs. My nephew Michael Brooks graciously gave me intellectual property counsel. Mary Laur, the copy editor for the Smithsonian Institution Press, made numerous worthwhile recommendations for ensuring the consistency of style and the readability of the text. My Regents' Professor research funds, for which I am grateful, enabled my field trips to Guatemala in 1992, 1994, 1995, and 1998. A sabbatical in 1995—for which I should like to thank Susana Maxwell, Dean of Social and Behavioral Sciences at NAU, and Clara Lovett, President of NAU—gave me the block of time I needed to finish the first draft of the manuscript. Special appreciation goes to my mother, Violet, and my late father, Marion, for their inspiration.

James D. Sexton

Introduction In the spring of 1970, when I was a graduate student at UCLA, Professor Clyde Woods, a tall, muscular ex-marine, marched into the classroom, pointed his finger directly at me, and asked, "Why aren't you going to Guatemala?" I replied, "Because I don't think my Spanish is good enough." But the idea of traveling to another country to conduct research in a different culture quickly intrigued me. After discussing the issue with my wife, Marilyn, I changed my mind and decided to quit my part-time job with Chevron and go for broke with my graduate studies. However, before we could finish the spring quarter in normal fashion, student demonstrations against the Vietnam war shut the university down. All classes were canceled.

One of my sharpest memories during the turmoil of that year was of sitting on a windowsill on the third floor of Haines Hall and watching a platoon of policemen in new riot gear with face shields on their shiny gold helmets double-time into the quad to break up a boisterous crowd of students near the flagpole. As the cops turned the corner in front of the stairs leading to the entrance of the anthropology and sociology building, one young man broke the glass of a box containing an emergency fire hose, yanked out the hose, pointed the high-pressure nozzle at the patrolmen, and began soaking them with water—a big mistake. The last two peace officers in the last two files broke ranks, grabbed the student, and began beating him with their billy clubs. Before the demonstration got uglier, the police broke it up by arresting the tallest participants. Bill Walton, a star basketball player, was among the first students the lawmen singled out, seized, and hauled away in a white paddy wagon.

I was not surprised by the tactics of the riot control police since in 1968 I had been called to active duty with the U.S. Army. In a crash course on riot control at Ft. Belvoir, Virginia, we had been instructed to isolate the tallest demonstrators— the natural leaders during civil disturbances—in order to contain the unruly behavior of a crowd. Later, my company and a large number of other army personnel were trucked into a parking garage in Washington, D.C., where we waited on alert, with weapons, in case a demonstration in the capital got out of hand. Fortunately, we were not needed.

I certainly had mixed emotions about the closing of the UCLA campus. During the time I lost in the army, participating in a war I thought was a mistake, my goal was to get through my tour of duty and return to graduate school. When I finally had the chance to re-enroll after a military leave of absence, I was a more serious student: eager to make up for lost time, excel in my studies, finish my degree, and obtain a teaching job. But the closing of the university presented me with another potential delay in my education. It was an easy decision to travel to Guatemala, where I could earn course credits for fieldwork among the descendants of the classic Maya. The magnificent cities of Tikal and Copán that these ancient people had built fascinated me. Their advanced scientific developments, such as the discovery of the concept of zero (the basis for modern mathematics) and the invention of an accurate calendar to promote their agricultural and religious practices, awed me as well.

Clyde had done his doctoral research in 1968 in San Lucas Tolimán, Sololá, under the direction of Benjamin Paul at Stanford University. Upon completion of his doctorate, Clyde was hired as an assistant professor at UCLA. He took his first team of student research assistants to Guatemala in the summer of 1969.[1] By the summer of 1970 his wife, Barbara, had given birth to twins, so Clyde elected to stay at home with his wife and children.

That season, Peter Snyder, another new professor at UCLA, went in Clyde's place. After completing his doctorate at the University of Colorado, Pete had worked for two years as a research assistant for a medical team from Stanford University, studying genetics among the Maya Indians who lived in the towns and villages surrounding Lake Atitlán. He was capable and willing to direct the next season of field research, which would begin on 23 June, the eve of the religious holiday of Juan Bautista.

On Saturday, 20 June, I arrived in Guatemala City on a Pan-American flight from Los Angeles. Being alone in a city where mainly Spanish was spoken was a unique experience. Having spent my first night in Guatemala City at the old but elegant Pan-American Hotel in Zone 1, my first sight of the Guatemalan countryside came from a front-row seat on a first-class bus operated by the Rutas Lima line. The company ran a safe, dependable service from Guatemala City to Quezaltenango with large, comfortable buses that had been manufactured in the United States. They were aging but well maintained.

At 8:00 A.M. sharp I boarded the bus at a station just up the street from the national library. After leaving the clogged, diesel-smelling streets of the capital, the bus headed northwest up the mountains on the Pan-American Highway. On either side of the road, as far as the eye could see, were country houses encircled by abundant cornfields. The land rolled endlessly but not as gently as the vast cornfields of Nebraska or Ohio. The terrain was more sharply undulant, having been tormented by volcanic activity and upheaval caused by underlying tectonic plates colliding over millennia. To the left of the bus were distant views of the peaks of El Fuego, Acatenango, and El Agua, volcanoes at whose northern feet lies Antigua, the colonial capital until earthquakes and flooding nearly destroyed it in 1773.

By 11:00 A.M. the bus had stopped at Los Encuentros, a settlement where the highway crosses a road that continues north to the Quiché town of Chichicastenango and south to the Cakchiquel towns of Sololá and Panajachel. In Los Encuentros I boarded a Dodge van, refitted with extra seats, and I headed south. Along the way the driver frequently stopped to let off or pick up passengers, usually women dressed in colorful, handmade blouses and skirts and men clothed in western shirts, trousers, and small fedoras. Soon the van was packed with riders speaking Spanish and *lengua* (a Mayan tongue). In our cramped quarters their sweating bodies, bathed in sweet-scented soap and covered with clothes saturated in wood smoke, emitted a unique musk of hair and skin—a smell not repulsive but deliciously exotic. Inside a net made of sisal, one woman transported a chicken, bound in such a way that it could utter only a muffled squawk when the bus hit bumps in the road.

Leaving Sololá, we began our descent, nearly straight down, to Panajachel. From each angle in the road to the right of the bus, my eyes embraced spectacular views of Lake Atitlán, with its huge body of fresh water reflecting serene images of brilliant green mountain ridges and three immense volcanoes. To the left of the bus, just below the village of San Jorge, we passed a crashing waterfall that emptied into the delta of the San Buenaventura *finca* (farm).[2]

In Panajachel I rendezvoused with three other members of the 1970 field school at the Maya-Azteca Hotel. The rest of the crew was to arrive later. Our fifty-cents-a-night rooms were equipped with nothing more than straw mattresses and cold water. We were all a bit apprehensive about our field assignments. We would each live in a designated town with an Indian family and spend half of our time writing field notes and collecting standardized interviews and the other half collecting data for our master's theses.

After taking frigid showers to rid ourselves of the sweat and grime from travel in the semitropical sun, to which our bodies were unacclimated, we gathered in one of the larger rooms to discuss our field conditions. Most of our worries focused on how we would stay in touch with our loved ones in the United States while living in homes with no electricity, no phones, and poor mail service. Around midnight the wealthiest student, who had brought both his wife and his surfboard in a new van he had driven down from Malibu, lit up a half-cigarette of marijuana. Most of us sipped from cold bottles of *gallo,* a popular but somewhat bland Guatemalan beer. In the wee hours of the morning, we all found our way to our beds for a noisy, restless night's sleep.

I was not as anxious as some of the other students since I had spent the previous summer in Vietnam. The helmeted national police of Guatemala, patrolling the streets in pairs in their light blue uniforms, and the rustic, primitive beauty of the countryside looked familiar. Guatemala had much in common with Vietnam. The majority of the people in both of these tropical countries were small-scale farmers of Asian descent with remarkably similar physical characteristics[3] and with well-developed oral traditions. They eked out a living in stunningly beautiful settings while suffering from governmental indifference and bearing the burden of increasing civil strife.

Yet there was an astonishing uniqueness to the land and people of Guatemala. In Vietnam the majority of the population were lowland Vietnamese (Viets), living in the delta and coastal regions and practicing Mahayana Buddhism. The mountain people, fewer in number, were a mix of several minorities, practicing animism. In Guatemala the majority of the people were a mix of different groups of Maya Indians, living in the highlands and practicing folk Catholicism, a curious blend of Catholic and indigenous beliefs and practices. In Vietnam the lowlands were the most scenic areas. Their bright green rice paddies bordered rural villages and coastal cities that were dotted with Buddhist pagodas. In Guatemala, while the hot, flat lowlands and coastal cities had their allure, the sloping uplands were the most breathtaking regions. Their jade-colored cornfields nestled around villages and towns that were marked by Catholic churches.

After the night at the Maya-Azteca Hotel, Pete Snyder took me out in his outboard motorboat to the pueblo (town) of San José la Laguna (a pseudonym), an hour's ride across the lake.[4] We observed fishermen patiently waiting in dugout canoes on the placid, early-morning waters for black bass to swallow the hooks attached to their lines. On the shore of the lake were terraced onion patches. Rising almost vertically from the lakeshore, the land was covered with fields of corn, beans, squash, and sisal and with coffee groves that were sometimes shaded by larger trees. Occasionally, brown spots marked rectangular patches of freshly hoed earth. Looking backward, I could see the Quixcáp and Panajachel Rivers spilling into the lake. As my eyes panned the scenery, I was captivated by the mountain walls enveloping the lake.

As we approached San José, I noticed wood smoke rising from the kitchens of traditional Mayan homes made of cane walls, straw roofs, and dirt floors. We secured the boat to the pier and walked up the dirt road leading to the town center.

I was to be the first anthropologist to carry out systematic fieldwork in San José. In exchange for 40 quetzales (then equal to 40 U.S. dollars) a month, a Tzutuhil family gave me room and board in their *sitio* (homesite). Late in the evenings I wrote my field notes by candlelight, kerosene lamp, or Coleman lantern. Often I could hear the relaxing sound of an accordion playing softly in the distance. Sleeping on the floor in my sleeping bag, spread out over an air mattress, was only a minor inconvenience. Each night before going to bed, I sprayed the perimeter of the sleeping bag with insect repellant to keep away scorpions and other unwelcome critters. I also surrounded myself with limbs of trees to discourage snakes from invading my quarters. Some nights my sleep was disturbed by a chain reaction of dogs yelping from one end of town to the other when a stranger passed through the area. Other nights my sleep was soothed by the steady patter of raindrops on the sheet metal roof above my head. The roof, however, did not have a ceiling, and I never adjusted to the moist, cold air blowing in from the lake at night. By the last week of my stay, I had developed bronchitis, which I treated with the tetracycline that the pharmacist at the UCLA Medical Center had provided as part of our medical kits.

The meals that my hosts served me consisted primarily of delicious black beans and thick, yellow corn tortillas that were barely twice the size of vanilla wafers. Both foods were grown in the soil of the hills and the terraced mountain slopes surrounding San José. Always, the beans and corn were served with rich, home-grown coffee. When eggs were available, my hosts would mix them with the tasty black beans. Rarely was I served beef or chicken, although one evening the pecked wing of a chicken that had been on the losing end of a hen fight ended up on my plate. As often as I could, I supplemented my meals with bananas and avocados from vendors passing in the streets, since San José had no regular marketplace.

By the end of my second week in the field, I had mapped all the households in San José and chosen a random sample of sixty that included members of all the religious faiths represented in the town. I had also selected a purposive sample of twelve additional Protestant families. To help me conduct my interviews, I hired a local assistant to walk around with me to the houses that were on my list. Unfortunately, however, he was unable to help me gain the confidence of prospective interviewees. After receiving three refusals in a row, I realized I needed a more persuasive aide.

The head of the household where I boarded said he did not want to go around town with me to ask for interviews. He had been an assistant for Pete's medical team from Stanford and had suffered social reprisals for his participation in the gringos' research. His enemies accused him of being a communist, threw rocks at his house at night, and stole clothing that was airing on his patio. (Later, rumors would surface that I, too, was a communist, but I responded by asking how this could be true when the previous summer I had been a soldier in Vietnam, opposing the communists. Because many *Joseños* [people of San José] listened daily to the newscasts about Vietnam on their battery-powered radios, my retort worked.)

Since my host refused to help me conduct the interviews, I asked him if he knew someone else who would. He recommended Ignacio Bizarro Ujpán (a pseudonym), who lived across a rocky, unpaved street from my hosts' *sitio*. When I approached Ignacio, who was nearly my age, I was pleased that he agreed to help, although I wasn't sure whether I would get the same reception with him as I had with my first helper. Fortunately, Ignacio was older and more respected in the community than his predecessor, and we had no more refusals. To my delight, Ignacio was a perceptive and articulate interpreter of his Tzutuhil Maya culture. I relied on him frequently to explain events that I was witnessing as well as those in which I was participating.

That summer I successfully collected all the data necessary for the general project and for my master's thesis. My initial field experience was so rewarding that I returned to Guatemala in the summer of 1971, this time as a teaching associate working mainly in Panajachel, where Clyde had his headquarters. We placed a Peruvian student in San José who also used Ignacio as an assistant. In addition to helping the student collect data for the overall project and for his master's thesis, Ignacio proofread our revised interview schedules and served as a model for demonstrating to the other students how to conduct interviews. Again, Ignacio's work was excellent.

Intrigued with Guatemala, I returned to Panajachel in the summer and again in the fall of 1972 to collect data for my doctorate. At the end of this period of fieldwork, I had plenty of information, but I knew it would take some time to write my thesis and to secure a teaching job at a university. Once I began teaching, I could not be sure of obtaining funding for more research, but I was certain I would be busy putting together new courses and trying to publish the data I had already collected.

Toward the end of my stay in 1972, I contemplated what I could do to give Ignacio employment while I would be back in the United States. One morning I came up with the idea of asking him to write his autobiography and keep a diary, tasks that not only would give him something to do but also would help me keep in touch with what was going on in his town and country. I was pleased when he agreed to my suggestion.

Before I left, Ignacio showed me his first pages in Spanish. They were promising, but in places they lacked sufficient detail and depth to merit publication. I encouraged him to write some more and to send the results to me. Meanwhile, I accepted a teaching position at Northern Arizona University in August of 1973, and I officially completed my doctorate in December of the same year.

At the end of the summer of 1974, Ignacio gave the first batch of his pages to another graduate student working in his town, who carried them back to the states and mailed them to me from Los Angeles. As I opened the manila envelope and pulled out the yellow pages filled with Ignacio's careful penmanship, I was excited. The sheets of notebook paper had the earthy aroma of Ignacio's *sitio*. In my spare time, I began translating and editing his words. Periodically, I received new material in the mail, and I collected more information on return trips to Guatemala in 1975, 1976, and 1980.

By December of 1981 the University of Arizona Press had published the first volume of Ignacio's life history, titled *Son of Tecún Umán*. The reception of the book was so positive that the Press sent me an unsolicited contract for a sequel in the spring of 1982. That year, at the end of my first sabbatical, I returned to Guatemala to gather more data.

By the summer of 1985, Ignacio and I had published the second volume, *Campesino*. In this book appeared a few folktales that Ignacio included as part of specific episodes of his life story. When I told him how much I liked these tales, he said there were lots of them and suggested that we do a separate book on them. In 1975 I had recorded a creation myth similar to the one in the *Popol Vuh* from Juan Sahon Martín, a shaman who performed a *viaje* (ceremony) for me in a famous cave just below San Jorge la Laguna. Realizing that I could combine Ignacio's tales with Sahon's myth into a book, I encouraged Ignacio to give me more stories to translate and edit, which he did. And I worked on the folklore book at the same time that I was working on the third volume of Ignacio's life history.

I returned to Guatemala in 1987 and twice in 1988 during a second sabbatical, when I also traveled to all the other countries of Central America. In January of 1992, the University of Pennsylvania Press released *Ignacio*, the third volume of the life history. Four months later, Doubleday Anchor published *Mayan Folktales*, which was so well received that Ignacio and I decided to do another book of folklore. I returned to Guatemala the same year to collect more tales.

In 1993 Ignacio agreed to serve in the office of *alcalde* (head) of the *cofradía* (religious brotherhood) of San Juan Bautista. In 1994 I returned to Guatemala during the titular fiesta of San José and secured a detailed account of his year's service in this prestigious office. This account will appear in the fourth installment of his life history, which is tentatively titled *Joseño*.

The following year, during the first part of my third sabbatical, I returned to Central America with my son, Randy.[5] From Guatemala City, we took an excursion to the Mayan ruins in Copán, Honduras. When we returned to Guatemala City, we took the Rutas Lima bus to Los Encuentros, as I had so many years before. There we switched to a refurbished Bluebird school bus so jammed with passengers that the fare collector could barely weave through the aisle. Finally, from Panajachel, we took a public launch to San José. There we met Ignacio and his family and observed the festivities of the titular celebration. On the return trip, an ice-cream vendor who had been working the crowds at the fiesta lifted his cart on deck and shouted, "Get your warm ice cream!" And many passengers did.

I collected more tales from Ignacio and continued translating and editing them during the end of my fall sabbatical and during the summer of 1996. By mid-June of 1997, I had completed *Heart of Heaven, Heart of Earth,* a second volume of thirty-three previously unpublished Mayan folktales. Its content not only complements *Joseño* in particular, but the tales and legends also expand our knowledge about the present-day Mayan world view in general.[6]

■ ■ ■

In the past twenty-eight years, I have witnessed a number of changes in the towns surrounding Lake Atitlán, many of which have been documented in Ignacio's diaries. Among the most notable material changes, there are now more men and women wearing western clothing; more electricity, running water, and televisions in the homes; more paved roads connecting the towns; more buses running on those roads, loaded with more people; more motorized launches carrying people across the lake; more schools with a larger number of grade divisions; more people competing for scarce land and jobs; and more construction of office buildings and homes, especially vacation houses of Ladinos (non-Indians) on or near the waterfront. Among the most noticeable nonmaterial changes, there are increasing numbers of people speaking Spanish rather than *lengua* and more converts participating in the activities of Protestant churches of various denominations.

During the early 1980s insurgency and counterinsurgency escalated in this region, often trapping the campesinos between two fires. The presence of military personnel in the towns and villages increased accordingly. By the beginning of the 1990s, the guerrillas had lost ground, and the army became less obtrusive. On 30 December 1996 a peace agreement was reached between the guerrillas and the army, but despite the commendable effort toward democratization, the real political power remains primarily in the hands of the military.

In spite of these developments—not all of them pleasant—there is much about the region that has changed very little. The overall charm of the people persists, and the general splendor of the land is the same.

Geographically, San José la Laguna is located in the midwestern highlands of Guatemala in the department of Sololá, which has a capital of the same name.[7] Sololá is one of Guatemala's twenty-two departments, which are similar to the fifty states that make up the United States. Along with the other six countries of Central

Map 1. Guatemala with political boundaries and location of Lake Atitlán.

America (Belize, El Salvador, Honduras, Nicaragua, Costa Rica, and Panamá; see Map 1), Guatemala is situated on a somewhat narrow stretch of land between the larger land masses of North and South America. Of all the Central American countries, Guatemala is the third largest in size. It is also the most populous, with some ten and a half million people, over half of whom are Maya Indians. In addition to being the most culturally diverse of these countries, Guatemala has the most striking topography, especially in the department of Sololá.

The most remarkable feature of the department of Sololá is Lake Atitlán, one of the most beautiful lakes in the world, whose body of fresh water continually changes color—from dark blue to turquoise to silver. The surface of the lake is about 5,500 feet above sea level, although the water level has been dropping slowly since the severe earthquake of 1976. On the southwestern shores of the lake stand the three towering volcanoes—Atitlán, which soars to 11,500 feet; Tolimán, which reaches 10,350 feet; and Nimajuyú (San Pedro to the Ladinos), which rises to 9,925 feet.

Concentrated on the agricultural land around the water are three groups of Maya Indians—the Tzutuhiles, the Cakchiqueles, and the Quichés—who live in pueblos and *aldeas* (villages) at different levels of development and with different percentages of Indians and Ladinos. Santa Cruz la Laguna, whose population is about 99 percent Cakchiquel Indian, is the least developed of these places, and Panajachel, whose population is 74 percent Cakchiquel Indian, is the most developed. (See Map 2 for the location of these towns and *aldeas*.[8])

This part of the world enjoys a cool tropical highland climate with two well-marked seasons: the dry season, from November through April, and the wet season, from May through October. The locals call the wet season *invierno* (winter). Around the lake, the climate is semitropical and of a monsoonal character. The temperature rarely drops below 50 degrees Fahrenheit, and this happens only very early in the morning. In the shade, the temperature rarely reaches 80 degrees, and when it does, it is in the middle of the afternoon (Sexton 1992b).

Although Spanish, the national language, is spoken in the department of Sololá, most people speak an Indian language as their native tongue. The three Mayan languages spoken around Lake Atitlán—Cakchiquel, Tzutuhil, and Quiché—have been classified into a broader linguistic group called Quiché, which is in turn part of the larger Mayance (Maya-Quiché) family.[9]

In addition to identifying with their linguistic group and with the nation as a whole, many rural Guatemalans identify closely with the town in which they live. Among the Indians, the town to which one belongs can be readily determined if a person chooses to wear the brightly colored, traditional costume for a man or a

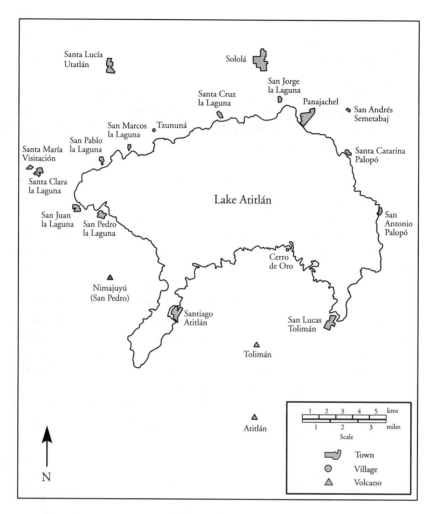

Map 2. Lake Atitlán with surrounding towns.

woman that is unique to each town. As a whole, women tend to be more traditional than men in their dress.

The family is the basic social and economic unit in Guatemala. Most marriages are monogamous, although it is common for a man and woman to live *juntos* (together), in a kind of common-law marriage. Although there are still younger family members who take care of older relatives, the trend is for a family to comprise the married couple and their children (a nuclear unit). Whether the newly joined couple lives near the parents of the groom or of the bride depends on the comparative wealth of each. If the couple lives with one of the parents after marriage, they usually set up their own kitchen (cooking hearth) as an independent unit. As soon as they are able, they establish their own home, although often not far from one of the parents, depending on the availability of land.

In the past kinship was traced through the father's side, but today it is traced through both the father's and the mother's sides, according to the national legal system of Guatemala. Surnames, however, are traced in a patrilineal fashion, with each child receiving two. The first surname, which follows the given name or names, is that of the father; the second is that of the mother's father. With given names, there is also the custom of naming a child after one of its grandparents. Although the grandparent after whom the baby is named may worry that he or she may be blamed if the grandchild dies (Sexton and Bizarro n.d.), there is also the belief that, as with corn, a person's life essence is transformed and regenerated after death in his or her descendants, which explains the practice of naming a grandchild after a grandparent (Warren 1989; Carlsen and Prechtel 1991; Carlsen 1997).

There is a tendency toward a division of labor by gender. Men do most of the heavy work in the fields. They also may work at secondary occupations as masons, bakers, and weavers on foot looms. Women cook, weave on back-strap looms, clean house, take care of the children, help weed and harvest the crops, and sell surplus vegetables and weavings in the marketplace. Although equal under the law, women are subordinate to men in a number of ways, learning less Spanish and traveling less than men. While they contribute equally to the well-being of the family and are consulted in most matters, their husbands often make the final decisions (Sexton 1992b).

While most of the campesinos are folk Catholics, a growing number identify with Acción Católica (Catholic Action, or Roman Catholicism) or with Protestantism. As in most of the religions of the world, the extent to which the tenets of Catholicism or Protestantism are followed varies with the individual. Members of both groups may retain some traditional beliefs and practices alongside those of their avowed faith. An example of this tendency is found in one of the folktales of this book, "The Gold and Silver Fish," in which a poor man and woman thank both God and the goddess of the lake for their good fortune.

Traditional elements of the world view also include curing, divination, concern with various gods and saints, and even occasionally witchcraft. Prevalent is a pantheistic view of the supernatural. *Dueños* (owners or gods) are still said to rule over land, hills, mountains, water, rain, wind, and other natural phenomena. Ancestors, gods, and Catholic saints are consulted in sacred caves. There is the belief that each person has an animal or a spiritual form called a *nagual,* and important persons might have more than one form that can be used on different occasions.[10]

Religion involves both public and private rituals that may include the offering of incense, blood, flowers, and liquor and the sacrificing of chickens and roosters. Public rituals also include richly dressing the images of saints and parading them through the main streets of the towns to the accompaniment of flute and drums as well as ensembles of guitars and wind instruments. These parades no longer end at the traditional ball courts for ritual ball games in which the losers might be sacrificed to the gods, but there is a strong passion for soccer games, which often cap major fiestas.

During the main fiestas honoring saints, dance dramas are celebrated in the streets, but in many towns their importance is fading, with even the most popular ones—such as the Dance of the Conquest and the Dance of the Mexicans—being discontinued. Younger men are not willing to undergo the expense of renting the costumes or to volunteer the time it takes to train for the dances and give the performances.

Religious syncretism is most evident in the *cofradías,* or religious brotherhoods, whose main obligations are to sponsor saints and to bury the dead. For example, when Ignacio agreed to become the *alcalde* of the *cofradía* of San Juan Bautista, he referred to this saint in a speech as at once the representative of God, the heart of heaven and earth (or the center of the world), and the *dueño* of rivers, storms, and hills. Ignacio said:

In the name of God, who is the heart of heaven and heart of earth, in the name of our fathers, who have given us a heritage, we ought to preserve and take care of our Mayan culture. Our fathers have bequeathed our culture in place of themselves—they have gone and have turned into dust, but their spirits are always with us. Also, we are going to die, but it will be our sons and our grandsons who will serve the representative of the heart of heaven and heart of earth, who is San Juan Bautista, patron and guardian of our town, a saint of god of the clouds and of the rain, who also is *dueño* of the origins of rivers and hills, a saint of god who also is *dueño* of the storms. And the image of this saint is what we are going to serve for a year. (Sexton and Bizarro Ujpán n.d.)

Although Ignacio's words suggest that the Christian god that the Spaniards introduced in the early 1500s is now a supreme god who encompasses the Mayan concepts of heart of heaven and heart of earth, two folktales appearing in this collection illustrate that the pre-Columbian deities are not forgotten. In "The Legend of Francisco Sojuel: A Tzutuhil Story," the hero offers *costumbres* (rituals) to the *dueño del santo mundo* (god of the sacred world, earth) as well as to the God of heaven and to the saints. In "Heart of Heaven, Heart of Earth: A Tzutuhil Tale," it is the precontact gods *Ruc'ux Caj* and *Ruc'ux Uleep* (Heart of Heaven, Heart of Earth) rather than the Christian god who are identified as the heavenly and earthly centers of the world.[11] It is likely that a number of present-day Maya see little difference between these Christian and Mayan deities.

While service in a *cofradía* is believed to help secure the favor of a saint, it also offers an avenue to social status and prestige and serves to redistribute wealth in a community. The *cofradías* have ranked offices, with the highest being that of the *alcalde.* And the *cofradías* themselves are ranked, with the one caring for the image of the patron saint having the most prestige.

Men climb the social ranks within a *cofradía* by periodically bearing a cargo, or office, for a year. As the men who hold office spend money on food and drink for fiestas that honor the saints, they may become poor in wealth but rich in social status. In more prosperous towns, however, the *cofradía* may function as a socially stratifying mechanism (Cancian 1965) because the wealthier families tend to get their sons promoted through the ranks more quickly and acquire the honorable position of *principal,* or town elder, who is consulted on civil as well as religious matters. Even Protestants, who generally reject both Roman and folk Catholicism, may express their respect for a *principal* by kissing his hand upon meeting him in the streets. Although a *principal's* whole family shares the prestige of his high status, his wife and children enjoy this status only vicariously. When their husbands hold office, women actively participate in activities such as preparing *atol,* the ritual corn drink consumed during celebrations in honor of the saints.[12] But if a woman actually has her own office, it is a low-ranking one called a *texel,* in which she plays a supporting role and often performs menial tasks such as serving refreshments during meetings.

Many Maya Indians know and hold a wide range of traditional beliefs, although the number of these beliefs accepted tends to decline with formal education. These beliefs include the following: Campesinos should pay homage to the *dueños* of the land before planting and harvesting and to the goddess of the lake before fishing in it or traveling over it. The distant sound of a child crying at night may be the spirit of someone who is going to die and thus a harbinger of death. Also, an owl hooting at night is an omen of death. The sacred winds of the lake will cause the death of sinners by drowning them. Fire is sacred and contains a holy spirit, and spitting on it results in a dry mouth for the spitter. Through sympathetic magic (Frazer 1963), fruit will become smaller in the next year's harvest if placed in the same basket with corn. A *brujo* may use personal items to bewitch a personal enemy or an enemy of a client. Misfortune is most likely to happen on bad-luck days and during bad-luck hours; Mondays, Wednesdays, and Fridays are bad-luck days, and midday and midnight are bad-luck hours. A person's general fate or *suerte* (luck) depends on the day on which he or she is born (Sexton 1992b). For example, a person born on the day of Bakbal (one of the twenty day-lords in the Mayan calendar, whose name means "night") will be afflicted by sickness and other bad things in his life. Never will he be able to achieve success in his endeavors. On the other hand, a person born on the day of Noj (another day-lord, whose name means "incense"), will enjoy great fortune.[13]

In addition to these traditional beliefs, there is the conviction that *secretos*, ritual or magical acts and objects, can protect a person from misfortune and can have a positive effect on a given situation. For instance, giving a boy leftover food is said to harm his development and negatively affect his memory, causing him to be forgetful when he grows up. A mother may counter the deleterious effects of leftovers by performing a *secreto*. Ignacio explains:

The mother grabs a half-burnt stick and begins to speak to the food. Suppose the boy is
called Manuel and yesterday's food is beans. Then the mother says to the beans,
"Yesterday's food, now Manuel is going to eat you. I ask you not to harm him when he is
grown. Don't numb his senses so that he will forget his machete, his hoe, his rope, or his
tumpline." The mother says these words with the half-burnt stick in her hand, positioned
on the food. After performing this *secreto*, the boy can eat the old food [with impunity].

Similarly, another belief is that a parent can stop a child from wetting the bed at night by doing a particular *secreto*. The mother collects little stones, has the child urinate on them, and then puts them into a sack made of *pita* (fiber from the agave plant). The stones are put on the hearth of the *temascal* (sweat house), where other stones are heated and water is splashed on them to generate steam. As the small stones get hot, the urine evaporates, and the afflicted child ceases to wet the bed at night. The persistence of such traditional beliefs among the modern-day Maya is evident from the folktales in this book.[14]

■ ■ ■

As I noted in *Mayan Folktales* (Sexton 1992b:xxii–xxiv), establishing the precise origins of folktales is problematic, especially when similar folktales appear in related but distinct cultural groups such as the Maya of Chiapas, Mexico, and the Maya of Sololá, Guatemala. What is more important than establishing the ultimate origins of a tale is examining the cultural content in the context of what these tales do for the people who tell them. Most of the tales in the present collection have a predominance of either ancient Mayan or contemporary Mayan elements. Other tales have mainly Ladino cultural elements, while still others reflect a clear mix of Mayan and Ladino cultural characteristics.[15] Regardless of the content, anyone can tell any of these stories whenever he or she thinks of it and has someone to listen to it. There are no special taboos against telling folktales (such as telling them only at a particular time of the day or of the year).

This collection of folktales and legends is particularly rich in providing insight into the beliefs and behaviors of the people who tell and listen to them. For example, these tales sanction social obligations to participate in religious festivals and to conduct *costumbres* in honor of various *dueños* of sacred places by offering them candles, incense, flowers, and other precious items, as illustrated in the tale "The Story of the *Tecolote.*"

Dreaming is an important vehicle for understanding the meaning of life, and many Maya believe that the gods may speak to women and men in dreams. In the "Story of an Enchanted Place, Paruchi Abaj," for instance, the *dueño* of enchantment appears to two hunters to tell them whether their offering to him was acceptable and whether they had permission to hunt. Also, the deceased may appear to loved ones in dreams, as in "A Sacred Story," in which a husband devoured by jaguars appears to his wife to tell her where his remains are. Finally, individuals may receive their supernatural callings through the medium of dreams, as illustrated in the tale of "Doña María and Her Three Children."

Also reflected in these tales is the belief that people can turn into animals, as in "The *Sombrerón* and the Blue Fly," in which a man transforms himself into a fly to visit the place of the dead. Supernatural beings such as angels who lust for beautiful, lifeless humans may turn into animals such as buzzards, as in "The Angels Who Were Eternally Punished for the Evil They Committed on Earth." Supernatural beings such as the devil may also turn into humans, as in the "Story of the Black God, *Dueño* of the Night." And in "The Man Who Wanted to Learn to Be a *Brujo* and a *Characotel,*" a supernatural entity appears in a whirlwind as a man with an ugly face and enormous teeth. The theme of humans transforming themselves into animals, and supernatural beings transforming themselves into humans and animals, is typically Mayan.

The tales also reflect a world view that includes *brujos* (witches) who cause people misfortune, such as illness, or who counteract the witchcraft of other *brujos*. *Ajkumes* (shamans) and spiritualists divine and cure. *Naguales* include winged creatures such as owls, eagles, and hawks and quadrupeds such as cats, mountain lions, and jaguars. Cats and owls have equal power to do bad things. *Characoteles* can use extrasensory powers to move utensils to scare people into dying, as in "The Man Who Wanted to Learn to Be a *Brujo* and a *Characotel.*"

The notion of *suerte,* which may be good or bad, is also an element of the world view found in the tales. For instance, the "Story of an Enchanted Place, Paruchi Abaj," reveals that rich people who don't treat poor people well during their life on earth have the *suerte* to go to the hellish place of Nima Sotz' (the big bat). The "Story of the Goddess of the Lake" shows that those who have the *suerte* to die by drowning may enjoy an afterlife with the goddess of the lake in a blissful place of gardens and flowers below the water—a variation on a theme that is widespread in Mesoamerica. Also, the power of a good-luck object may work for one person but not for another, as in the case of "The Two Brothers and the Fortune." Finally, the "Story of the Owl" illustrates that a person who harms owls will have bad luck. When a man wounds an owl for making too much noise, he consequently must face the *dueño* of Pulchich Hill, a fat man with an angry appearance.

In these stories there are also explanations for the creation and nature of animals and supernatural beings. For example, in the "Story of the Dog and the Cat," the action of a creator accounts for the behavior of wild animals such as jaguars, bears, and mountain lions. It also explains the behavior of domesticated animals such as dogs and cats. In "A Sacred Story" we learn the origins of the *dueño* of the clouds and the *dueño* of darkness. In "Doña María and Her Three Children" there is a similar account of the origins of the *dueño* of the clouds, or rain, as well as the *dueño* of the wind and the *dueño* of the cold. Although the content varies with each story, themes of creation are widespread in Mayan folktales.

Two stories offer competing explanations for the existence of the black and white races. "The Angels Who Were Eternally Punished for the Evil They Committed on Earth" shows an angry father causing one of his sons to turn black for laughing at him when he was passed out, nude, on the ground. In contrast, the "Story: Everything was Created" offers an account of how Heart of Heaven, or Grandfather, and Heart of Earth, or Grandmother, were not satisfied with the black and white races they created and on their third try succeeded in creating man and woman in their own brown image. Although the details vary, the theme of the creation of black, white, and brown races is found throughout native America.

These tales also serve as a mechanism for relating historical events. For example, the "Story of the Emigration and Tragedy of a Cakchiquel People" is a historical narrative of the arrival of people in San Marcos la Laguna. It also describes early conflict with established groups such as the Tzutuhiles. "The Legend of Francisco Sojuel: A Tzutuhil Story" relates the defiant exploits of a famous shaman of Santiago Atitlán who, among other things, is able to drink three gourd jars of moonshine and remained unfazed. "The Grandfather and the Faultfinders" is a story about the constrictive effects of meddling people and about a priest who takes up the habit of traveling by donkey in the countryside. Finally, the "Story of the Señor of Esquipulas" relates how the Maya were forced by the Spaniards to abandon their culture and forget their gods or suffer savage tortures, such as having one's breasts or penis and testicles severed.

These stories reveal much about the natural habitat of the region, especially its plants and animals. In the tales we learn of plants such as *güisquiles* (chayotes), corn, *ayotes* (gourds), *camotes* (sweet potatoes), yuca, pumpkins, peaches, and wheat—the latter two of which were introduced by the Spaniards. Also appearing in these tales are such creatures as owls, bats, jaguars, mountain lions, bears, wolves, coyotes, pigs (imported from Spain), paca, raccoons, snakes, opossums, birds, chickens, ducks, mice, monkeys, deer, wildcats, blue flies ("eyes of death"), burros, bulls, horses, spotted cavy, armadillos, mountain pigs, coati, *taltuzas* (rodents that carve long tunnels in the earth), and *tepescuintes* (brown rodents with black stripes on their backs). There are also nonlocal creatures such as sharks, whales, and even elephants, which of course are found only in zoos in Central America. In general, the tales suggest, everyone should be kind to animals—even hunters, lest they be punished for wounding them by the *dueño* of the animals, as in the "Story of a Hunter."

In addition to mention of real plants, birds, mammals, and insects, we find in these tales information about magical objects and supernatural images and beings. In "The Fisherman and the King," for example, we discover that a young fisherman can perform astonishing feats such as breathing under water because of his magical ring. In this story, the young fisherman also captivates the animals of the forest with the hypnotic sound of the indigenous drum and *chirimía* (wind instrument similar to an oboe). In "The Gold and Silver Fish," the singing goddess of the lake rewards a woman with a magical fish that transforms itself into silver and gold and fills a coffer with money. In the "Story of the Señor of Esquipulas" we learn of the consequences of deceiving the Holy Christ. And in the "Story of Maximón" we see that even unsanctioned saints have powers such as that of immaculate conception.

These folktales reinforce cultural values such as honesty, generosity, uprightness, and proper social behavior. Godparents, who are often wealthy Ladinos, play an important role in family and social relations even when language barriers are cause for humorous interactions, as illustrated in "The Story of the *Tecolote*." But in "The Gold and Silver Fish," while luck brings fortune to a subordinate Indian family, the goddess of the lake punishes a rich, envious *comadre* (co-mother) and *compadre* (co-father) with poisonous snakes for their deception and avariciousness. In "The *Sombrerón* and the Blue Fly," liars, witches, prostitutes, and envious people are whipped by men in the afterworld of the *dueño* of death. Trying to please all of one's social critics may be too confining, as illustrated in "The Grandfather and the Faultfinders." And in the "Tale of the Teacher," another story dealing with misguided criticism, a pompous teacher learns humility when he must depend on an untutored boatman he has castigated to save him from drowning. In other words, everyone has his or her worth.

Foolishness is cause for both scorn and laughter, as illustrated by the local episodes of the half-wit Simón in "Simple Simón." On the other hand, cunning is rewarded, as in the exploits of clever Señor Adrián, who obtains fruit, avoids being recruited into the military, and evades a vagrancy law by his wits. In his triumphs, he generates a lot of laughter and ridicule aimed at the wealthy and powerful.

Filial respect and obedience pay off in "A Sacred Story," in which humble people are spared the wrath of God. Small rocks and a gourd jar magically save them from hunger and thirst. In contrast, filial disrespect and disobedience—even to a selfish father—can have grave consequences, as in the case of "The Rich and Miserable Man: A Cakchiquel Story." Not only must one be respectful of his elders and ancestors, but if he wishes not to suffer dire consequences, he must also properly honor supernatural beings, as illustrated in the "Story of an Enchanted Place, Paruchi Abaj."

Some of the folktales that reflect Ladino cultural elements, or a blend of Mayan and Ladino traits, illustrate popular Guatemalan proverbs.[16] In "Temperament and the Deeds of the Son of God," the people who encounter a wandering, poor, humble man reap what they sow. Those who are gracious and kind to the son of God are blessed with bumper crops, while those who are spiteful and mean to him are cursed with calamity. In other words, *Quien siembra vientos cosecha tempestades* (He who sows winds harvests storms).

Another popular saying, *El que mal hace mal espera* (He who evil makes, evil awaits), is illustrated in "The Louse Who Caused the Death of the Womanizing King: A Tzutuhil Story," in which a ruthless king who sends men to battle in order to acquire their wives as concubines suffers his own misfortune. The same tale emphasizes the saying *Agrado con agrado* (One favor deserves another) when the townspeople offer to give the mouse and the louse food in exchange for their help in fighting the king. Thus this story explains the behavior of the louse, who has the right to suck the blood of humans; the mouse, who has the privilege to eat part of their crops; and the rabbit, who has the liberty to eat vegetables.

The "Story of the Señor of Esquipulas" reinforces the adage *Vuestro sí, sea sí, and vuestro no, no* (Let your yes mean yes and your no mean no, or do what you say you are going to do). In this case, a man and his wife suffer when they promise to visit the image of a saint but do not. "The Woman Who Died for Three Days and Went to Get Acquainted with Hell" demonstrates the maxim *Cuando la muerte llega, no pide edad, posición o sexo* (When death arrives, it doesn't ask age, position, or sex) by telling of a woman who dies rich in material goods but poor in social status. And "The Man Who Wanted to Learn to Be a *Brujo* and a *Characotel*" highlights the proverb *El valor es solo una virtud cuando se deja dirigir de la prudencia* (Valor is only a virtue when it allows itself to be directed by prudence, or prudence is the better part of valor). In this tale, an apprentice's training becomes too dangerous to continue.

Finally, an analysis of these tales illustrates that they are to be enjoyed not just for their educational value but also for their humor, which at times borders on the macabre, blasphemous, and *colorado* (vulgar). In "The Story of the Assistants Who Worked with the Germans," for example, workers from the underdeveloped Indian town of Nahualá take their jefe literally when he asks them to bring him more heads (individuals) for work. In "The Oldest Tale of My Town," a priest puts a curse on his parishioners after they whip him for farting during a mass. In "The Louse Who Caused the Death of the Womanizing King: A Tzutuhil Story," a louse punishes a despised king by biting him on the *culo* (ass) and *pipe* (penis). In "The Nuns and the Charcoal Vendor," the last tale of the book, a charcoal vendor belittles a policeman who orders him to make his burro lose an erection in front of nuns.

Folktales

Heart of Heaven, Heart of Earth: A Tzutuhil Tale

A Tzutuhil tale goes like this.[17]
Our fathers, the old Tzutuhiles, were peaceful men. They didn't like war because they possessed great wisdom about how to do things [without resorting to war]. They were dedicated only to making sacrifices in the hills and the volcanoes, invoking the Heart of Heaven and the Heart of Earth, called in Tzutuhil *Ruc'ux Caj, Ruc'ux Uleep.*

The story says that the Tzutuhiles of great powers disappeared in the air, in the clouds; they went below the lake; they disappeared in the volcanoes and in the hills by their own ability without the help of spirits. They had in their brains, in their blood, and in their bones their own ability to become invisible when they wished to do so.

When the Spaniards began the conquest, killing many Quichés, Mames, and Cakchiqueles, the Tzutuhiles formed a single group and met in order to think and speak. They met in a place that was called Chuitinamit, now called Santiago Atitlán, on the shore of Chinimayá, now called Lake Atitlán. They could have opened a front for a bloody war against the Spaniards because there were many of them who had the power to disappear in the air, in the clouds, and to go below the lake.

Then the story goes that those who had this power said:

Indeed we can make a stand against the Spaniards for a bloody war because there are many of us Tzutuhiles who possess the power to disappear in the air, in the clouds, and below the lake. We know that we have the power to walk in the air and in the clouds and nothing will happen to us, but it's a shame that we will lose many of our people— our women, our children, and our grandchildren. We cannot allow our race to be terminated and to stain the greenery of the ground with our blood. Let us use our intelligence and wisdom.

Then the story says that an *ajkum* [shaman] and Tzutuhil prince called Ajpop Achi spoke to all those who were gathered:

I am an *ajkum* and Tzutuhil prince. My voice has been heard by *Ruc'ux Caj, Ruc'ux Uleep* (Heart of Heaven and Heart of Earth), and they tell me, "It is better that we disappear in the air, in the clouds, below the lake, in the hills, and in the volcanoes. When the *itz'el tak' winak* ("demons," the Spaniards) arrive on our land, each is to use his power. Those who don't have this great ability will remain, but there will not be a war."

The story says that everyone agreed. When the Spaniards invaded the Tzutuhil lands, many of our Tzutuhil forebearers didn't want to spill their blood; they left of their own power. Many of them disappeared with their own families. Now they say they are in the clouds, they are in the hills, in the volcanoes, and they live under the lake. Before leaving they said to those who didn't have this power:

You won't be alone. Nothing will happen to you. We will be with you by day and at night, now by means of the air, by means of the clouds, and by means of the thunder of the volcanoes. The Spanish devils will search for us in order to kill us, but they won't do anything to us. We will be with you. You won't be alone, nor will you be orphans. We will leave you but with the understanding that we must be remembered by day and at night. Then by day and at night we will be with you. The Spaniards, children of the devil, will never kill you.

So it was when the Spaniards arrived in these lands. The Tzutuhiles of great powers—that is, the *ajkumes,* the *naguales* [persons who can turn into spirit forms], the *brujos* [witches], the thinkers, the clairvoyants—had already disappeared voluntarily. Now they say that they are living below the lake. They are in the air, in the clouds; they live in the volcanoes and the hills. Moreover, for that reason, among us Tzutuhiles, the custom is believed and preserved that when a person goes on a trip or to work, be it in the early morning, during the day, or in the night, upon leaving one's house, he with his hand offers a kiss in air, remembering and saying, "*Nataá, nuteé, watit, numamaá* (fathers, mothers, grandmothers, and grandfathers) of us, the Tzutuhiles, accompany me in the sorrows, in the sufferings, and in the happiness of this day or night." The person offers a kiss with the hand to the air because he believes that our forefathers are present. And if the person departs over the lake, upon getting into a canoe, he grabs water with his hand and kisses it, saying the same words, "*Nataá, nuteé, watit, numamaá* who are under the lake, accompany me." A person also does this when he is going to the hills and to the volcanoes.

The story says that when the people leave their houses, if they do not do these remembrances—if they don't entrust themselves to the Heart of Heaven [and] the Heart of Earth and to their forefathers—that is when the bad hour strikes them. They drown, fall in the ravines, and die in accidents or of sudden death.

Valerio Teodoro Tzapalíc, a Tzutuhil of Santiago Atitlán

Story of the Goddess
of the Lake
Long, long ago lived many families in San José who were devoted to making their living by selling fish in Sololá and in Panajachel. They say that when they first began [to sell fish in these towns] they went on foot, but for them it was very tiring and they suffered because the path they took was very steep and slippery in the rainy season. In time they grew weary of walking and thought it better to buy canoes. Then only a few people walked, and the majority went by canoe to cross the lake. In each canoe rode ten to twelve persons, rowing to reach Jaibal or Panajachel.

One time, the story says, twelve people left in a canoe, and in the middle of the lake they encountered a strong whirlwind that came from the north and swept them along in the canoe. They say the people struggled to save themselves, but there was nothing they could do. The whirl of air was too strong, and the canoe capsized.

Of the twelve people who went in that canoe, eleven drowned. Only one was able to survive. The only survivor was found on the rocky beaches of Santa Cruz three days later. It was he who related everything that had happened on the lake. He said that they went rowing very calmly; they were in the middle of the lake when suddenly came a strong whirl of wind that blew from north to south. But he said that in that strong wind appeared many men, women, and children, as if they had been swept away by the wind, as if they had been carried by the whirlwind. The rowers lost control of the canoe, and it capsized. At once eleven people drowned, among them women. He said that the men, women, and children who came in the whirlwind were not real people, only ghosts or spirits. (It is believed that they are the spirits of the people who die in the lake, or, better said, the spirits of the people who drown in the lake. They are the ones who turn over canoes. It is believed that those spirits are not happy, that they are alone in the lake. They need more companions, and that's why they overturn canoes and drown others.)

Of these eleven drowned persons, not one of their bodies was found. The people say that they struggled to recover the people who drowned, looking on all the shores, but they could not find a single body and got tired of looking for them.

They say that in that accident eight children lost their *mamá* and *papá*. They could not decide what to do about their inheritance because their parents left some belongings: land, houses, and money. Seven of the siblings planned to distribute the inheritance without considering the youngest brother. They treated him like a stranger, dispossessing him of their parents' house.

The seven very content siblings kept the property—land, houses, and money. But the youngest brother cried by day and at night. He felt very sad for all that they had done to him. He had to abandon the house of his parents and to request shelter with other families. But the story says that the boy never forgot about his parents. It was difficult for him to get through the days and nights.

One night the boy fell asleep in his shelter. In his dream appeared his mom and dad. And in the dream they said to him, "Son, why are you sad for us? Don't be sad for us or for the inheritance. Your brothers took advantage of our property. There will be no problems. We continue to live below the lake; we have not lost our bodies. Always, we will be looking after you because you are our son."

When it dawned, the muchacho began to remember everything that he had dreamed and began to cry again. The boy didn't eat, nor did he think about working, only about his mom and dad. The second night, when he was sleeping in the same shelter, he dreamed again. He dreamed he was walking on the shore of the lake, passing by the beach of Santa Cruz, when suddenly he saw his mom and dad coming. In the dream, the boy felt a great fear, but his parents spoke: "Son, now don't cry anymore because if you continue crying, soon you will be with us. We have not died. We are alive and we are at the service of the goddess or *dueña* [owner, lady] of the lake. Be careful and cry no more. Think about your life. We are alive, but we cannot live together. For we three to live together, you will have to come with us."

The following day the boy got up and began to remember the dream that he had had for a moment. Then he headed for the place where he had spoken with his parents in the dream. He went walking, passing through San Pablo, San Marcos, and Tzununá, going all along the lake shore, but he ran into some boulders where it was difficult to pass. The boy struggled to climb the big rocks. When he was passing, he saw sitting amid some boulders a very beautiful señorita of a very fine appearance. She was neither white nor brown nor blonde. Her face looked blue and transparent. She had green eyes, very fine teeth, and long, white hair like silk. She was wearing a lot of jade necklaces and gold rings. And she spoke to the boy, saying, "Young man, where are you going? What are you doing here? People don't come to this boulder. It is a sacred place. I'm the only one allowed to be here because I am the *dueña* and goddess of the lake. I make the wind move over the lake, and I do a lot of other things."

The youth replied, "I have come to take a stroll. Some months ago my *mamá* and *papá* drowned in the lake, and I'm very lonely for them. Without my parents I don't have peace in my life. Twice I have dreamed that I chatted with my parents in this place, but it was only a dream."

The goddess of the lake said to the muchacho, "Young man, your parents have not died. They live with me. Why are you sad for them? They live more peacefully with me. If you would like, you can see them."

The young man said, "I feel sad for my *mamá* and *papá*. My siblings distributed the inheritance without giving me anything, and that is why I cry by day and at night. I cannot eat or think about work. I only think about my parents and my life because my siblings tossed me out of the house like a stranger. That's why I have come here, to relieve my solitude."

The story says that the goddess of the lake said to the boy, "Come with me. We're going to see your parents. Without a doubt they want to see you."

The boy didn't want to go because he knew that his parents had died. But the goddess of the lake made the boy go with her.

The youth had to obey the woman, and he followed her. Suddenly the place was changed, with a road going down. The road had many turns, but all the sides were planted with many flowers, beautiful flowers.

When they went walking, the story says that the woman began to sing a very beautiful song that no person could sing, and the echo of her voice and their footsteps were very well heard. It was as if they were walking on a beautiful carpet. Finally, the story says, they arrived below, seeing many houses, good houses, and seeing many gardens with innumerable flowers. The woman said to the boy:

Young man, we have arrived here in this place where I am the goddess of the lake. The people who are said to have drowned live with me. They are alive; they have not lost a single hair. In this place live your parents, and really you can stay here for a while so that you will forget the loneliness and the sadness that you feel for them. Tell me when you want to return. I will take you back to the place from which I brought you. Here you may eat and drink with your parents with much ease.

The story says that the woman continued walking and singing and entered into a beautiful house. Far away was heard the echo of her voice, a voice soft and fine.

The boy began to see many people—men, women, and children—walking in the gardens. It was very pleasant. Many women were making tortillas, others cooking little tamales, and yet others cooking food. When the food was prepared, he heard the sound of a bell calling everyone to eat. Many people began to arrive there, among them the mom and dad of the youth. Then they recognized one another and greeted one another. When the boy wanted to kiss the hands of his parents, he could see the forms of their bodies well, but when he tried to grab their hands, they were only images. They did speak, however.

They told the boy not to cry anymore; if he wished, he could live with them. The boy told them everything that had happened with his seven siblings. His parents told him he shouldn't think about the inheritance anymore; the better inheritance was for the three of them to live together. The muchacho told them, "*Papá, mamá,* you already died. You drowned in the lake when you were traveling in a canoe. Now I have seen you and talked to you. Now I want to go back. The goddess of the lake brought me here when I was going for a walk on the shore of the lake."

"Fine," the dead ones said. "It is certain that when we came to this place there were eleven of us, and all of us are in the service of the goddess of the lake. Here, we are under the lake, but we are not suffering at all. Here, there is joy without end. Many of us are working in the gardens, many are doing the cleaning, others the cooking. They called us to eat."

Then, the story says, they sat down and were served hot little tamales and other food in wooden baskets. The dead ones very happily began to eat. They offered food to the boy, but when he wanted to eat—that is, when he wanted to grab the little tamales—they were not real. They were just images. When he wanted to grab the basket of food, it too was only an image. So the boy could not eat. But he saw that the dead ones ate well, as people like us eat.

When the boy saw these things, it gave him a great scare and a strong chill in his whole body. In a little while he saw nothing, and the place changed. Then he realized he was with the goddess of the lake again. She asked the boy if he already had seen his parents and if he had chatted with them.

The young man answered yes.

Then the goddess of the lake took the muchacho on his return journey. She went singing very happily, passing among the most beautiful flowers, but now it no longer was the same road. It was another road.

It could be seen well that they were below the lake, but the water did not harm them. They went very calmly. When they got to the shore, the goddess of the lake told the boy, "Here we are. Here we will say good-bye. Let me give you a kiss."

"Fine," said the youth, and he accepted the kiss. The boy felt it well when she kissed him.

"Now you can kiss me," said the goddess of the lake. The boy began to tremble and didn't have the nerve to kiss her. But the story says the goddess requested him to give her a good-bye kiss. Finally, he mustered the courage to kiss her, but when he wanted to embrace her to kiss her, there was only air. It wasn't a woman, and at that moment the goddess of the lake disappeared.

The story says the boy remained motionless for a moment. Little by little he recovered his strength, and before he realized it, he was situated on the rocks of Cerro de Oro, on the other side of the lake. But the boy had first encountered the goddess of the lake on the rocks of Santa Cruz.

The youth went to the town and related to the people everything that had happened to him. A little later the young man disappeared. He did not get sick, nor did he die. It was a mysterious disappearance. Now it is believed that the young man lives with the goddess of the lake. Many people say that in the early mornings they have seen, passing by the shores of the lake, a pretty woman. Also, many times they have seen a handsome young man, crying on the shores of the lake. But when the people wish to approach them, at that instant they disappear.

Don Bonifacio Soto Bizarro (85 years old) and
Benjamín Bizarro Temó (72 years old)

Tale of
the Teacher
One time, a schoolteacher had such bad luck that he had to work far away from the city, and to his sorrow, he had to travel a long way on foot and to cross a large river. Along the way, he got hungry and very thirsty. When he passed a small store, he wanted to buy something to quench his thirst, but in this store there were only *naturales* [natives]. They could not speak Castilian [Spanish], and the teacher could not speak *lengua* [the native tongue]. The owners of the store got frightened when they saw the teacher arrogantly and presumptuously speaking in Castilian. But the poor *indígenas* [Indians, indigenes] did not understand what the schoolteacher was saying, and they were as quiet as mutes.

The schoolteacher angrily said, "You frightened Indians, are you dead? Why can't you understand and speak Castilian? I, on the other hand, can speak, read, and write, and I lack for nothing. I can go anywhere in the world." [Then he left the store and headed toward the bank of a river.]

When he came to the edge of the river, he took a rest, not knowing what was going to happen to him. Then along came a skipper (of a boat), and the teacher said to him, "Muchacho, can you take me to the other side of the river?"

"With great pleasure, señor, but you have to pay me because it costs me for the passage," he said.

Well, the teacher pretentiously stepped into the boat and put on a pair of dark glasses. Then the skipper began to row, and the teacher said to him, "Muchacho, you are a good rower, but can you read and write?"

The poor rower answered, "No."

"Poor one," said the teacher, "you have lost half your life just like a blind person. All you can do is row this humble boat."

When they were halfway across the river, suddenly there was an imbalance and the boat (canoe) overturned. The poor rower began to swim in order to escape death, but the presumptuous teacher could not swim. He was at the point of drowning when the rower said to him, "*Maestro* [Teacher], you say that you know everything. Well now, help yourself and start swimming. Otherwise, you will lose your whole life. I, on the other hand, still have half of my life." [And he swam to the bank of the river.]

"Son of God, help me. Without your help, my life is lost!" yelled the teacher.

At last, the skipper took pity on him and jumped back into the river to help him. When the teacher realized his life had been saved by a blind and ignorant person, he said "*Gracias* [thanks], brother, you have saved me from this river. You are very brave. If we had both been teachers, our bodies would be floating, and we would be food for the fishes. Now I realize, brother rower, that there are things one man can do that another cannot."

And they said good-bye as if both were teachers, because each one possessed [worthwhile] knowledge.

Colorín colorado,[18] this tale has ended.

Ignacio Bizarro Ujpán

The Story of a Tzutuhil Named Adrián from San Pedro la Laguna

This is the story of a Tzutuhil named Adrián from San Pedro la Laguna who died about ten years ago. He did not know how to read or write, but he was a very clever campesino. This tale is based on reality. Many people from San Pedro, San Juan, and other towns tell the tale of Señor Adrián.

It is said that one time a female *characotel* [person who turns into a *nagual,* or animal form of a person or spirit, and acts as a spy or does evil] was persecuting the sick mother of Adrián.[19] He was not afraid of *characoteles,* and one night he decided to follow the *characotel.* He had discovered the path that the woman used when persecuting his sick mother, and he did not want to wait for the *characotel* to come to his *sitio* [homesite] again to bother his ailing mother.

Señor Adrián told his mother, *"Mamá,* tonight I shall go to look for the *characotel* who persecutes you during the night."

His mother said to him, "No, son, do not go out, because the *characoteles* are evil. I don't want you to suffer because of me. I am old. Instead, let the *characotel* pursue me until my death."

But Adrián decided to go look for the *characotel.* So he painted his face with charcoal, covered himself with an old sweater, and stood on a street corner. When the *characotel* was approaching, Adrián went to stand in the middle of the street. The *characotel* fell to the ground, trembling with fear, and she could not get up. She thought that she was seeing the *dueño* [owner, god] of death or some evil spirit. Adrián said he felt very pleased when he saw the *characotel* down on the ground, trembling with great fear.

In truth, there was no street light, but there was clear visibility from the light of the moon. And this is how the *characotel* saw the face of the ghost-man who was in the street. They say that Adrián also threw himself to the ground and rolled over to where the *characotel* was, and then he stood up. The *characotel* was on her knees and did not say a single word but merely trembled from the cold. Without speaking, Adrián took the *characotel* away in the darkness and had sex with her. Afterward, she returned to her house, shivering from the great cold she felt. Adrián said he [almost] died of laughter at having had intercourse with the woman *characotel.*

The woman *characotel* had such bad luck that she barely made it back to her house because of the fright she had experienced. On the following day, she woke up with a high temperature and trembling all over her body. Then the people next door arrived to visit, and she told them what had happened. Some told her she had seen a demon. Others told her that the *dueño* of the *negros* [blacks] was the one that caused her situation. They say that nine days later she died.[20]

Another time, they say that in a certain village there were some beautiful *jocote* [hog plum] trees that had ravishing fruit, which made a person want to eat them. But the owners were very fierce and had some dogs that were just as brutal as they were. No one could enter into this *sitio* because he would fall into the hands of the owners and their dogs. Every time the dogs barked at night, the owners would come running out to capture anyone who dared to enter the *sitio.*

Then, it is said, Señor Adrián had a craving to eat *jocotes,* and he tried to go into the *sitio.* But he could not because the dogs came out running and barking. Then he looked for a way to tame the dogs. When he returned a second time, he took some bread and fed it to them. That way, he became a friend to the dogs, but he did not try to enter the *sitio.*

He returned a third time and did the same thing. He gave bread to them. By this time, the dogs were his friends, and he very calmly climbed the *jocote* tree and began to pick some of the delicious *jocotes.*

It was like this for a time, but at last the owners found out what was happening because when they arose in the morning, there would be *jocotes* strewn under the trees that Señor Adrián had dropped during the night. Then the owners prepared to trap the thief. They readied a rope to tie him up and sticks to give him a good beating.

Then it is said that the thief arrived and gave bread to the dogs, and when he was climbing the *jocote* tree, he discovered that a candle was lit inside the house. He then got down and went to listen to what the owners were saying. Inside, the owners said, "When we hear any noise, we will go out to tie up the thief and give him a good beating." The thief (Adrián) was outside listening to what the owners were saying, and he did not try to climb the *jocote* tree again. Instead, he went back to his house.

The following day, Adrián prepared charcoal and got some old, torn clothes ready. At nightfall, he painted his face with the charcoal and set off for the *sitio* where the *jocotes* were, with his face painted black and wearing the old, torn clothes, finding his way by moonlight. Then he threw a rock against the *jocotal* [tree or plantation of *jocotes*] and remained on his knees on the patio of the house, making a cross with his hands on his chest.

When the owners heard the noise of the thrown rock, they got up rapidly with the sticks and ropes to capture the thief. But when they opened the door, they saw that on the patio of the house was a strange body with torn clothes and a black face. The owners of the *jocotal* received a great shock and did not notice when they threw away the sticks and ropes. They locked themselves in the house, trembling with fear.

Señor Adrián said that he very happily climbed the *jocotal* and filled his sack with ripe *jocotes.* He said that is what he did every night. Upon arriving, he would throw a rock against the *jocotal* to see if the owners would come out. But he said that every time the owners heard the sound of the rock being thrown, they would get on their knees and stay inside the house for their protection, so that the evil would not penetrate the house. But this was no evil; it was just the *jocote* thief.

Señor Adrián was a poor man who had no money and who barely had enough to feed himself and his wife. But it is said the *cangrejeros* [crab fishermen] would leave early to catch the crabs in the lake. At two in the morning they would gather maguey *pitas* [fibers made from the agave plant], and at three and four o'clock in the morning they would go to the shore [of the lake] in their canoes. On the shore they would gather wood and make a campfire in order to warm themselves a bit because it was very cold. Afterward, they would return again to check the *pitas*.

It is said that Señor Adrián had a craving to eat crabs, but since he did not have any money, he looked for a way to frighten the *cangrejeros*. Then one day, he arose at three in the morning and said to his wife, "For sure, we are going to eat crabs." But he did not have on any underwear, and he put on only his *mashtate* [loincloth] and set off for the shore of the lake.

When he arrived the *cangrejeros* were warming themselves by the campfire they had made. Then Adrián took off running down the dock and jumped into the lake for a swim. When the *cangrejeros* heard the sound of footsteps on the dock and the sound of something hitting the lake, they got frightened and thought that it was a ghost or an evil spirit. They ran toward their homes, leaving their canoes with the crabs. When Adrián saw that the owners of the crabs had run off, he very calmly came out from the lake to the edge of the water. He chose the large crabs and put them in his sack and contentedly returned to his house.

It is said the *cangrejeros* returned to the shore of the lake but only after it was morning because they were very frightened. But it had not been a phantom or an evil spirit; it had only been Adrián, the crab thief.

Another time, the story says, [*camineros* (roadmen)] were constructing the Cocales road, extending it to San Lucas Tolimán. *Pedranos* [people of San Pedro] and *Juaneros* [people of San Juan] were obliged to work very hard, and they ate only as God would help them. Each group would work fifteen days, and when it was Señor Adrián's turn to work, he would take only enough food to last him for two or three days. This was not because he did not want to take more food but because there was not enough food in his house, and he was obliged to perform the work.[21] Adrián had to use cunning in order to get enough food to complete his work assignment.

One afternoon when Adrián was working in the area of Pampojilá *finca* [farm, plantation], which is scarcely four kilometers from San Lucas Tolimán, he asked a lady to do him the favor of lending him her son. Then, the story goes, the lady gave Adrián permission to take her young son with him to San Lucas.

Well, Señor Adrián went with the young boy, and when they were about to enter the town, he said to him, "I will pretend to be blind. Take my hand and lead me to the houses to ask for alms of the people. Warn me when we come to ditches, rocks, or other places where we cannot pass."

Adrián put on torn clothes, and, furthermore, he said to the boy that if the people should ask, the boy should say that he was Adrián's son, he had eight brothers, and his mother had died. That was what the boy would say.

Everything went as planned, and when they entered the town, Señor Adrián allowed himself to be taken by the hand of the boy so that the blind person (Adrián) would not trip over rocks. They went into the houses, asking for alms. The people gave them tortillas, bread, money, eggs, and food.

The people would ask the señor if he had been born blind or if [his blindness] was due to illness. He would answer, "It is because my wife died. I was left with eight children, and because of crying over the death of my wife, I lost my sight. Now I am an invalid." The people with great compassion would give him money. When [Adrián and the boy] had filled their sack with provisions, [Adrián] carried it, but he could not walk very well because he was pretending to be blind and suffering a lot.

When they had left the town, he changed his clothes, and they were very happy. When they arrived at Pampojilá, he gave some money and part of the provisions to the young boy, and he still had a lot left for himself. It is said that Adrián did not keep everything for himself but that he shared his take with the other poor people from San Juan and San Pedro; that is, the food he had gathered he would divide with the other workers. He would do this often, and the people would say that this made them happy because he would help them out. He was the only one who would do these things.

During the administration of [President] Ubico, it is said that it was prohibited not to carry the *tarjeta de vialidad* [*libreto,* card (passport) that proved one was not a vagabond]. Many were jailed by the police for not carrying it. The *Pedranos* and *Juaneros* would often sell their products in the markets of Mazatenango and Retalhuleu. Señor Adrián was one of these.

On one occasion, the mounted soldiers were at San Bernardino Suchitepéquez, asking the people for the *vialidad.* Señor Adrián did not carry this document, and [he knew that] those who did not would surely go to jail. On this trip, Adrián asked his companions if they carried that document. They said they did carry it, but he did not. Then he said to his companions, "Only God knows that I forgot to bring the *vialidad* card. If I am thrown in jail, please let my wife know."

At the registration stand, people were waiting in a long line to show their identification. Señor Adrián went into the sugarcane field to disguise himself. After putting his pants, shirt, and sombrero on backward, he asked his friends to please tell the authorities that he was deaf and dumb. When his fellow travelers identified themselves to the policemen, Adrián pretended he could not hear or speak. The policemen grabbed him and asked him for his *vialidad,* but he did not answer. He merely began to turn around and around and act as if he were dying of laughter. Then the policemen said, "This is a crazy deaf and dumb person," and they let him pass. After traveling one kilometer, Adrián rearranged his clothes and acted normally again. His companions on the trip were surprised, but for Adrián it was a game.

When they passed through San Antonio Suchitepéquez, it is said that in that town they were recruiting people for the military, without regard for whether they were married or single, only looking for people with strong bodies.[22] Since Adrián had a robust body, he told his companions on the trip, "Muchachos, please take my bag when we are going through the pueblo, because I have to walk alone. Further down the road, past the pueblo, I shall wait for you. Now, if they grab me, I shall have to stay in the barracks."

As he was going through the town, he very calmly put his arm and hand inside his shirt, acting as if he were one-armed, and with his other hand he carried a stick and hobbled as if he were lame. The recruiting patrol thought he was disabled and did not approach him. He calmly passed. At the end of the town, he was waiting for his companions and was dying of laughter. His companions returned his sack, and they went back together.

Another time, they say that Adrián went to San Pablo la Laguna. When he was arriving at the town, he saw some beautiful fruit: oranges, limes, and *jocotes*. But this man preferred the *jocotes*. He sat under the *jocotal* to see if the owners were guarding it. Since he saw that no one was at home, he climbed up the *jocote* tree to pick the ripest fruit.

He was doing this when the owners returned home and told him, "Damned *Pedrano,* you are the one who is always stealing the *jocotes,* because we are always losing fruit." The father and his sons—that is, the owners—cut some branches with which to beat the thief. The father said to his sons, "We shall give a beating to this wretched *Pedrano,* and we shall imprison him."

"Good," said his sons. They prepared the sticks, and they ordered Adrián to come down from the *jocote* tree.

Well, Señor Adrián very worriedly began to climb down, but two meters before he reached the ground, he suddenly jumped from the *jocote* tree and fell to the ground, acting as if he had received a mortal blow and turning over and over on the ground. Then he lay still like a dead person. The father and the sons (the owners) got very frightened when they saw the man was dead. They took off running in order to hide and avoid responsibility for the death of the man. But in truth, Adrián did not die. He did it only to frighten the owners. When he saw that no one was after him, he arose calmly and returned to the *jocotal* to fill his sack with the delicious *jocotes.* Calmly, he returned to his pueblo.

Another time it is said that Señor Adrián went to work on the coast. When he returned to his town, he carried a quantity of maize, climbing up the slope from Cutzán to Atitlán, then walking from Atitlán to San Pedro. But they say that Señor

Adrián now felt very tired. He arrived at Xecruz, eight kilometers from San Pedro. Suffering from exhaustion and hunger, he could no longer travel. Night fell as he sat beneath a tree. With nightfall, however, the coyotes came and wanted to eat the señor. Out of fright, he climbed the tree and trembled in the dark.

Below the limbs of the tree, hundreds of coyotes began to bite the trunk and scratch at its roots. They wanted to throw him out of the tree. Señor Adrián took off his *faja* [cloth band serving as a belt] and tied himself to a branch of the tree so that he would not fall into the mouths of the coyotes. He was trembling with fright, but since he felt very tired, sleep overcame him. He felt safe because he was tied to the branch with the belt.

The coyotes wanted the señor to come down. While the señor was sleeping, some rats ate through the *faja* with which he was tied to the tree. Just as Don Adrián hit the ground, his weight killed the biggest coyote, but without Adrián's knowing what had happened. The rest of the coyotes, when they saw that the biggest coyote had died, went running into the forest. Señor Adrián sat next to the dead coyote. Later other coyotes arrived, but they didn't come close. Without doubt the animals thought that he would kill them. But the coyote that he killed wasn't killed because he had intended to kill it. Rather, it was because the rat ate the *faja* and Adrián accidentally fell on the coyote.

Another time, the story says, Señor Adrián was working as a municipal policeman. At night, the guards and municipal police had the habit of cooking *güisquiles* [chayotes], corn, yuca, and sweet potatoes—whatever they could get.

In a place close to the Patziapá Farm, a señor and his daughter had sown a lot of *güisquiles,* pumpkins, yuca, and corn. But on the farmland they had built a *ranchito* [small, rustic house] where they could spend the night and guard the crops.

[One day] Adrián told the rest of his companions, "Today, *muchá* [muchachos], we are going to cook something to eat," but his companions told him that they had nothing. He told them, "Let's go rob the place near the *finca.*"

"No," said his companions. "We cannot because the señor and his daughter sleep there."

"Take the nets. I know what I'm going to do," he said. The muchachos took the nets, and they went in a canoe so that it would be easier. When they arrived on the shore, Señor Adrián put on a *traje de bailador* [dancer's suit]. He also put on a pair of shoes, placed a sword inside his belt, and covered his face with a mask of Don Pedro de Alvarado [Maximón]. Then he said to his companions, "I'm going to knock on the door of the *ranchito* so that the owner will become frightened. When I knock on the door, you begin to pick the *güisquiles* and ears of corn, as many as you want."

And that is what Adrián did. He walked up to the door of the *ranchito* and knocked. When the old man got up and saw a stranger at the door, he woke his daughter and said, "Get up—let us get on our knees and pray. Don Pedro de Alvarado has come to visit us."

And that is what they did. They got on their knees, offering incense in the manner of adoration. Don Pedro de Alvarado pulled out his sword and began to walk in front of the little house, making signs with his head that he was receiving the *costumbre* [ritual] that they were offering him. In their prayers, the *viejito* [old man] and his daughter asked many things of Don Pedro de Alvarado, but it wasn't Don Pedro. It was only Adrián and his companions stealing the fruit. When Adrián left, his companions already had the bundles of fruit in the canoe. And the story says that Adrián [nearly] died of laughter.

Another time it is said that on the 25th of July, Señor Adrián and his señora said they were thinking of going to the fiesta of Santiago, but as they had no money, they didn't go. Señor Adrián said to his señora, "I am going to go to the *mojón* [landmark] between San Pedro and Santiago [Atitlán] to look for a little herb and to see if I can get some peaches." In the jurisdiction of Santiago there are many peach groves; it is the crop of the *Atitecos* [people of Atitlán].

Then Señor Adrián left, taking a cape (overcoat), some charcoal, and a pair of glasses he got from a friend of his. When he was close to the peach groves, he could see that there were a lot of *Atitecos* guarding the trees. He hid to see if the guards would leave, but they didn't because they knew that robbers always came to this place.

With the charcoal, Señor Adrián made a mustache and a beard, and he put on the cape and the glasses. Then he approached the owners, but he kept a little distance from them. Seeing something strange, the owners became scared, asking each other what it was that they were seeing. One said, "Today is the fiesta of the apostle Santiago. Without doubt he is visiting."

Señor Adrián began to walk very close to the peach groves. The guards were scared even more, saying that they were seeing the patron saint. They ran to advise the town that they had seen the apostle.

After the owners ran away in fear, Señor Adrián happily began to pick the most beautiful peaches, taking as many as he wanted. Then he returned very contentedly to his house.

These episodes are based on real events. We Tzutuhiles always tell the deeds of Señor Adrián.

Ignacio Bizarro Ujpán

Story: Everything
Was Created

Heart of Heaven is Grandfather, father of our fathers. Heart of Earth is Grandmother, mother of our mothers, who also represents Mother Earth.[23] Long, long ago only they existed, Grandfather and Grandmother, and nothing more. Only the two existed. It was very peaceful. There was no shouting or sin in the world, but it was not happy. There was no one other than Grandfather and Grandmother.

The spirit of Grandfather was mysterious. He was not seen; better said, he was in heaven. The spirit of Grandmother was also mysterious, moving over the earth and seas. But there was no one to honor or remember them.

Then one time Grandfather went down to earth to talk with Grandmother. "What are we going to do to see a change on the earth and in heaven?" For centuries and centuries there had been only the two of them, and now they were old folks. They planned to create a son and a daughter so that they, when grown, could give them praise and honor them.

Then Grandfather took dry lianas and a good handful of beeswax and shaped it in the form of a boy doll. The lianas are what now are called bones. Now, the beeswax is called flesh. Thus was formed the doll of liana and wax. But it did not move. Grandfather told Grandmother to hit it with three lashes so that the doll of liana and wax would change into a boy. And so it was. But Grandfather and Grandmother thought it better to form a little girl so that there would be two. Then they made a little female doll of just wax, and with that they created woman. The following day there now were two, a male and a female, but they were little blacks.

And this is how the first blacks were formed. Because blacks were created first, they turned out to be very robust, tall, and strong.

Grandfather and Grandmother, however, were not happy with their first work. It is certain that they had not wanted the two little *negros* [blacks], but now they were unable to do anything about it. Once and for all, they had been created.

Again Grandfather went down to earth to tell Grandmother to form two more children; that is, to make two children who were not blacks. They didn't want to make them of lianas and wax again because if they did they would turn out to be blacks again. They thought a lot about what they would have to do. Then Grandmother began to grind some plants that had spikes, which are now called wheat.

So it was. Grandmother ground the wheat. From the milled wheat came a very white dough, and with that they formed two little dolls. Then Grandmother caressed them and gave them breath. Then they began to speak, but they didn't walk. Then Grandmother hit their feet with *chichicaste* leaves [nettles], and then they began to walk.

And this is how the *blancos* [whites] and *rubios* [blonds] were formed. They turned out to be very big and tall, but because they were made of the dough of wheat, they couldn't tolerate being in the sun.

But Grandfather and Grandmother had doubts about their second works. They did not turn out to be as they had wanted, because Grandmother and Grandfather were neither big nor tall, neither white nor blond.

Then Grandfather and Grandmother planned to have a son and a daughter like themselves; that is, with their own color and height. They didn't want more blacks, whites, or blonds.

Again, Grandfather went down to earth to tell Grandmother, "Grind yellow corn, and with the dough, form two little dolls."

"Fine," said Grandmother, and she began to grind yellow corn. When it was ground, she formed two little dolls with the dough. Then Grandmother caressed them and gave them breath. Then the two little dolls began to talk, but they did not walk, nor did they grow as the others had grown.

Grandmother got angry and ran to cut branches of *chichicaste*. She hit the two with branches of *chichicaste* all over their bodies. Not until then did they grow and begin to walk, but they didn't grow as the first two works had grown. The son and daughter made of yellow corn were not very big or tall, nor were they whites, blonds, or blacks. The son and daughter made of the dough of yellow corn turned out to be the Maya. Because they were made of yellow corn, the faces of the Maya were not white or blond but copper-colored.

Since we Indians were created after the others, we turned out to be shorter and smaller. We eat a lot of tortillas because we were made of the dough of corn. We are also very angry from the pricks of the *chichicaste* that we carry in our blood.

In contrast, the blacks are very tall and robust because they were the first work of the creation. And the whites and the blonds also are very tall and big, but because they were made of the dough of wheat, they are sensitive to the sun. Also, because the whites were made of the dough of wheat, they nourish themselves with bread and cereals, unlike us Maya, who eat only tortillas.

Colorín colorado, this short story has ended, arranged by a Tzutuhil *Joseño.*

Ignacio Bizarro Ujpán

A Very Old Story
[of Creation]

It is said that long ago there was no coast or high plateau from the shore of the Pacific Ocean to Quezaltenango and Santa Cruz del Quiché. It just was mountains, hills, and rocks. Then God decided to level everything from the shore of the ocean to Quezaltenango and Santa Cruz del Quiché.

God looked for a pair of persons who were very old. The man was called José and his wife was called María. The two were very poor but obedient. They had only a horse.

Then, the story says, God spoke these words to them:

I want it to be level from the shore of the ocean to a distance beyond, so that all the people will be happy. But you shall do this task. You shall do as I command.

Then God ordered:

Today, when night falls, leave the pueblo. Take the horse. Before sleeping, give him sufficient grass and tie two stones on the horse, one on each side of its back. Then you can go to sleep. At dawn of the next day, take note that you will be in a level place. Keep traveling until night falls, and do the same thing until completing everything.

"Very well," said the two old persons, and they began the work.

The story says that the next day, in the afternoon, they left their house, but very sad because they were very old. When night fell, they prepared enough grass and tied the stones on the sides of the animal. Then they went to sleep.

When they got up the next day, where they were had been transformed into a very level place. They became very frightened and got down on their knees [to pray] because they had witnessed a strange phenomenon.

The story says that they began to travel again, and when night fell, they did the same thing. The following day they saw a miracle. The plain was bigger than the day before.

Thus it was. They continued traveling, and each night that they slept, at daybreak there was a bigger plateau. The more days they traveled, the bigger the plateau.

Over time, however, they arrived in a place where it was very cold. They prepared the grass the same way, but there wasn't much of it, and the horse did not get full. At sunrise, there was not as much of a plain as after the other nights because the horse did not get enough to eat.

The following day the old people continued on their way. Already they had traveled a long distance from the ocean. Night fell, and they prepared the grass for the horse, but the horse didn't want to eat. It felt tired since all the previous night it had carried the rocks [without enough nourishment]. This night, when the old man tried to throw on the stones, the horse kicked him twice in his *huevos* (testicles), and with this he died, leaving the old woman alone.[24]

By herself, she was unable to fulfill God's command to level all the terrain. For that reason, they say, there now exist both a coast and a high plateau.

This has ended, and everyone eat lunch.

Zacarías Zea Suluí[25]

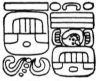

Story of a
Hunter
One time [there was] a hunter who lived on a *finca* [farm] named Montequina. This man was a servant of the *finca*. With the money that he earned, he bought a shotgun and some hunting dogs. Little by little he became a good hunter, taking with him his colleague. They went out at night, and every night they carried home animals. But [eventually] he thought it better to abandon his comrade. Thus it was with the man who became a good hunter on the *finca*. His best companions were the dogs and the shotgun.

Then the hunter got the idea to sell the meat of the animals he hunted. He would leave in the nights and on Sunday in the day. The dogs would chase the animals from their dens, and the man would pursue them with his shotgun. At times his hands failed and he only wounded the animals, such as raccoons, spotted cavies, armadillos, wild pigs, and coati.

But the *dueño* [owner, master] of the enchanted hill got very, but very, *bravo* [angry] because he was the *dueño* of all the animals that had died; that is, all the animals the hunter had killed or left wounded when his hand failed with the shotgun.

Then the *dueño* of the enchanted hill said, "My animals are being exterminated. Who will be able to heal the wounded? And the damned hunter continues to come to this place. Now I am going to punish him." Then he gave an order to a snake to bite him so that he would stop hunting.

One Sunday the hunter came with his shotgun and his dogs to the same place, as usual. The dogs began to bark. Then he aimed his weapon and shot at a wild pig. But the hunter's hand gave way, and he was unable to kill it.

The hunter walked a little more, when suddenly his foot fell inside the hole of a *taltuza* [rodent that carves long tunnels in the earth] and at once the snake bit the man on the foot. Then the serpent spoke: "My master ordered me to give you this painful bite, but you are not going to die. This is only a punishment so that you will not continue to come here." The reptile said only this.

The man swelled all over his body from the venom of the snake. They had to carry him because he couldn't walk. When he was at home, he told his family that a snake had talked to him. All his family felt a tremendous fright.

Over time, the bite of the serpent healed, and he continued hunting animals. It was Holy Thursday when he went again to the hill, Chuamango. He very contentedly took his shotgun and dogs, without giving any importance to what had happened earlier. In a while the dogs began to bark. When the hunter saw that many animals were coming, he aimed his rifle. He wanted to shoot, but the shotgun failed. He was very scared because there were many animals and he was unable to kill any. What he did was to return to his house. Then he told his family what had happened.

On Good Friday, the hunter didn't feel content being in the house. He grabbed his shotgun and left with his dogs. Still, his woman told him not to go to the mountain because it was a very sacred day, but he paid no mind to her. When he arrived at Chuamango, the dogs ran ahead barking and the man continued. As he followed the yelping of the dogs, suddenly his path was blocked. He could go neither forward nor backward. In the blink of an eye, the mountain looked like a city. The poor hunter was in the presence of the *dueño* of the enchanted place, a señor with white hair. He spoke to the hunter, saying, "Many of my animals have been lost because of you, and the wounded cannot be healed." The owner of the enchanted place grabbed his whip, which was the serpent, and gave him twenty lashes, saying, "Seventeen, eighteen, nineteen, twenty. You will be here to pay your bill. You will leave the shotgun and the dogs here [with me]."

As before, in the blink of an eye, the hunter was in the same place again [his original surroundings in the forest]. Sad and pensive, he returned to his house without the shotgun and his dogs. He told his family what had happened.

Seventeen days after having received the twenty lashes, the poor hunter fell sick with a fever. On the eighteenth day he was serious, on the nineteenth day he was in agony, and on the twentieth day he died. This is what the *dueño* of the enchantment had meant: "Seventeen, eighteen, nineteen, twenty. You will be here to pay your bill."

When the hunter died, many people remained sad because there wasn't anyone else to sell them meat. Before they put him in his box [coffin], his wife dressed him in his clothing, tied his head with a scarf, and put on his old *caites* [open-toed sandals]. The family was very sad, thinking that he had paid with his life for all the damage he had done on the mountain.

Days later, the woman of the man went to the enchanted place to see if by chance she could find the shotgun and dogs of her deceased husband, but she could find nothing.

Twenty days after the hunter died, a man went to Chuamango to look for firewood. Suddenly, he heard some shouts as if someone were running. He stopped making firewood. He looked and saw a man descending, whom he recognized as the hunter who had died. The poor woodcutter got very frightened. The hunter asked him, "My friend, are you making firewood?"

The man didn't want to respond. He felt afraid.

But the dead one continued talking: "My friend, talk to me! Don't be afraid. Please tell my wife that I'm here in this enchanted place, paying my debt for the animals I have killed, but I'm tormented by wounded animals. The *dueño* of this enchanted place told me to cure them. But I am unable to do anything, and for that reason, I'm suffering a lot."

The woodcutter mustered the courage to speak and said, "Hombre, we buried you in the cemetery. I was even one of those who carried you to the cemetery. For that reason, your woman will not believe that you are here in this place."

The dead one told the woodcutter, "So that my woman will believe that I'm here, take my scarf with which she tied my head, and take her my *caites*."

The man grabbed the scarf and the *caites,* trembling with fear, and he returned to his house without carrying the firewood. When he arrived at the house of the widow, he gave her the scarf and the *caites* and said, "Your husband, whom we buried twenty days ago, is in the place where he hunted a lot of animals."

The woman recognized the scarf and the *caites* and began to cry. She called everyone who had seen her tie the scarf on the head of her husband and put on his old *caites*. Everyone trembled with fear. And the poor woodcutter died within three days.

Colorín colorado, this story has finished. He who told it needs a little chocolate for another tale.

Lorenzo Pérez Hernández and Ignacio Bizarro Ujpán

The Two Brothers
and the Fortune

A story goes like this. In a town there lived a very poor family. When the parents died, they left their orphaned children neither money nor land—only the clothes they were wearing and a door and window made of wood that were attached to the *ranchito* [rustic house] where they lived. The *sitio* [homesite] where the *ranchito* was constructed belonged to a moneybags. The two brothers, after the death of their parents, were living for a while in the *ranchito,* but neither of them worried about their life, always living in laziness. On a certain day, the owner of the *sitio* told the two brothers to vacate the site; if they refused, he would hand them over to the law.

Well, one day the two brothers agreed to abandon the *sitio* and the *ranchito.* They thought about dividing the inheritance their parents had left them before dying. The older brother took the wooden door and the younger brother took the wooden window and they said, "To each his own, with his life and his fortune as God helps him."

They didn't go together, to see which of them would be the one to gain a fortune. The older brother took the wooden door; his hope was to sell the door in order to get some money to buy clothes and food. He passed through many towns offering the wooden door. One day passed, two days, and by the third day, nobody wanted to buy the door. This man now felt tired and very hungry, but he wasn't able to buy food.

In the afternoon of the third day he arrived at another town offering the door, but still no one wanted to buy it. There was such bad luck in this town. They told him that he should be very careful because very close to the town there were many thieves who had assaulted many people. Many had died because of the thieves.

The poor man was very scared, not wanting to leave the town yet but not having money to pay for an inn. He decided it better to leave the town in order to sleep in the countryside, since in the countryside he didn't have to pay for anything. The man carrying the door reached the woodland very afraid. Now, with night approaching, he arrived beneath a beautiful tree and said, "I will stay here and sleep under this tree." He prepared to stay there because he could no longer bear the weariness.

When night fell, he heard the uproar of the wolves and coyotes nearby. The poor man was frightened, and he couldn't figure out what to do. He said, "If I continue traveling the thieves are going to kill me, and if I remain beneath the tree the wolves and coyotes are going to eat me." Finally he decided to climb up the lovely tree, carrying the door, saying, "God spare me tonight." He put the door on a branch of the tree, and he seated himself on another branch. This is how he was when, about 10:00 P.M., four very tall, blond men arrived beneath the handsome tree. They carried extremely sharp machetes, which they arranged in the shape of a cross beneath the tree. Then they lit four candles, and they began to shoot dice.

The poor fellow, looking below at what the four men were doing, was very frightened, but he couldn't get down because he would be delivered into their hands. One of the four went to bring a sack of money that they had hidden, and they began to count it, saying, "This is all we have managed to get today. Tomorrow we will have to steal some more so that each one of us can have his own sack of money." That's when the one in the tree realized they were the thieves.

They continued with their wagering while the poor fellow watched from above. But this poor fellow was suffering and was tired of being on the branch of the tree. Besides, he had an urge to pee that he could no longer bear. Finally he urinated and the urine fell on the ground as if it were drizzling. The thieves said that it was drizzling, and as such they continued playing without giving importance to the pee that fell on them.

The man in the tree said, "This is the last night of my life. I can no longer withstand my weariness, but if I go to sleep, without doubt I will drop from the branch of the tree. The thieves will cut me to pieces with their machetes. Lest they kill me, better that I scare them." He threw the wooden door below, and it fell on top of the four robbers, who received a great blow in addition to the scare it gave them. They thought that a piece of the sky had fallen. Without noticing that it was [just] wood, they took off running, leaving the sack of money and the four machetes.

The poor fellow got down contentedly from the tree and carried off the sack of money and the four machetes. The only inheritance that he had been left was the wooden door, which now enabled him to acquire a great fortune. The following day the four thieves returned to the place to see what had happened to them the night before, but when they arrived they found only an old wooden door. They didn't see the money or the machetes.

When the poor fellow returned to his native town, he bought land, built large buildings, and had a happy family. After a time, his younger brother arrived to tell him that he had not been able to sell the wooden window, that he had passed through many towns but no one had offered him even a single quetzal for it. Then he asked his older brother to give him the address where he sold the door he had inherited because now he lived better [having parted with it]. Then the older brother told him: "The truth, brother, is that I am a bit better off, but not because I sold the door. The same thing happened to me—I was offering it in many towns, but no one wanted to buy it. What I did with my door allowed me to frighten four thieves who were under a tree."

And the younger brother said, "Please tell me what happened so I can do the same thing."

"Very well," said the older brother. "Take the wooden window and offer it in the towns where I went. I know that no one is going to buy it. Then, on the third day, when afternoon falls, go outside the town. Nearby there is a beautiful tree. When night falls, you will hear the noise of the wolves and coyotes. Then climb the beautiful tree, carrying the window with you. When the four men arrive, first pee on them and then throw the wooden window down. The thieves will flee, and you can bring back the fortune very calmly."

"Thanks, brother," said the younger brother.

The following day he was very happy. He took the window and passed through the towns where his brother had passed. No one wanted to buy it. On the third day he went through the last town, and they warned him, "Be very careful because close by there are many thieves." The man became very pleased when they told him that there were many thieves.

At sunset he left the town, looking for the tree of fortune, and he arrived right under the lovely tree. There he sat waiting for the uproar of the wolves and coyotes.

After a while the coyotes and wolves began their howling, and the happy man climbed up the tree to wait for the arrival of the thieves. They arrived, began to shoot dice, and started to count the money that they had stolen during the day. The man watching from the tree said, "This money is my fortune, and I will give you a great surprise." But he forgot about urinating on them. He was too anxious to have the money, and he threw the window down. Unfortunately, it didn't fall on the thieves, and this time they saw that it was not the sky falling, that it was only a wooden door. They realized they were being tricked again. They climbed up the tree, lowered the man down, cut him to pieces with their machetes, and fed him to the wolves and coyotes. This was the great fortune of the younger brother.

Colorín colorado, this tale has ended. It is not a common tale. He who wrote it is a Tzutuhil who lives on the shore of beautiful Lake Atitlán, Sololá, Centro-américa.

Ignacio Bizarro Ujpán

The Angels Who Were Eternally Punished for the Evil They Committed on Earth

This story is very old. My grandmother Isabel Soto [who died at 104 years of age] always told it to us when we were young children, mainly at night when we were ready to go to sleep. It goes like this.

Long, long ago there was no sin on the earth. Because all of the people feared God, they were respectful. They didn't steal or slaughter—violence was unknown. Everyone loved one another as brothers [and sisters]; there were neither poor nor rich. Everyone was equal. It is said that evil was born in the following manner.

There was a man who had two sons. He and his two children dedicated themselves to the cultivation of corn, beans, vegetables, and fruits of many kinds. One day, the story goes, the father of the boys wanted to experiment with something in his life. Then he began to crush sugarcane and beautiful apples. After crushing a big handful, he put it in a clay pot for one week. When he took it out of the pot, he sensed an agreeable aroma. Out of curiosity the man drank it. It tasted very delicious, and he began to drink and drink without knowing the effect. The man got drunk, and his two children were surprised because it was the first time that their father acted like this.

And it is said that this is how the same man made *chicha* [corn liquor]. He made it out of fruit, and because of this, *chicha (cusha)* is now made of fruit and corn. Then every day this man drank the ferment of fruit and corn.

On a certain day he got too drunk without realizing it. He went to pee behind his house, but after urinating he lost his balance and fell down. He remained lying down, naked, behind his house.

Then one of his children went to see his father, who was asleep and unclothed. This son began to laugh at the nudity of his father, and he ran to tell his older brother so that he too went to see his exposed father. But the older child reprimanded his younger brother and told him that he should have more respect for his father. Then the older child closed his eyes and covered his father. He didn't want to see the nudity of his father; he remained respectful.

When the father of the two children got up, he went into the house and asked his older son what had happened to him. The older son answered that his younger brother had been disrespectful. When he saw the father asleep and exposed on the ground behind the house, he laughed at him. Then the father got very angry with his younger son and told him that all his life he would have to go in search of work through many places in the world, scorned by his brothers, without rest, and having nothing more than hate and contempt. And it is said that when the father of the boy said these curses to his son, in this same moment the color of the boy's face changed, becoming black, and at the same time he was thrown from the house of his father. Meanwhile, the older brother received the blessings of the father; he became much more lightcolored than before.

The *viejitos* [old people, elders] say that because of this there are whites and blacks in the world. Then discord was born between the blacks and the whites, and there began the battle between brothers. The blacks began to kill the whites, and the whites began to kill the blacks. Daily, there were deaths on both sides. They say that all of the younger brother's children were born black and that the children of the older brother were born white. Because of this, the whites and the blacks don't like each other, but the blacks have more resentment because of the contempt they had for the father.

God, tired of seeing so many sins in the world, because there were many dead, one day made the judgment to terminate the sinners from the earth. God chose a town where both whites and blacks lived but where there was little evil, so the town would be like the seed of the earth.

Then God made the judgment about the earth. Suddenly a heavy rain and a wind fell, so strong that it broke branches and uprooted trees that fell on the houses. Many people died beneath the rubble and drowned from the rain. Only the town that did not have a lot of sin was spared. Because it was saved, there still exist whites and blacks. And the people of this same town were aware of all that had happened in the world [during the judgment].

Some days after the judgment, God sent angels from heaven to see if justice had been served. The angels came down to earth, but they committed vice. While they traveled around, they saw among the many dead a lot of beautiful, lifeless women. They lusted for them and sinned. Since the world is very large, the angels drew out their stay many days to accomplish their mission, but from so much walking they felt hunger. Because there was nothing else to eat in the world, the angels from pure necessity ate the flesh of the dead in order to satisfy their hunger. From that point, they could no longer fly to heaven, and they turned into buzzards, unable to speak anymore, able to say only, "*Utz-tii, utz-tii.*" They wanted to say, "How good the meat is!"[26]

The *viejitos* say that this is the reason that buzzards eat dead people and dead, spoiled animals—as eternal punishment for having eaten the flesh of the dead who died in the judgment. Because of this, the buzzard is the most contemptuous animal in the world.

Isabel Soto Toc

The Man Who Wanted to Learn to Be a Brujo and a Characotel

This tale is [about] a deed that happened to my friend Quique [short for Enrique] Miguel [a pseudonym], the same one who told it to me. He has a few years on me, but now he lives in the capital city of Guatemala. He was born in San Martín la Laguna [a pseudonym], but his father was a *Joseño* [person from San José]. Quique Miguel comes at times to see his relatives and friends. He speaks Spanish a lot because he has lived many years among the Ladinos. When he comes, he always talks to us in our Tzutuhil language, and he likes to tell his story, which happened in his youth. Now he is a member of Alcoholics Anonymous. And he told it to me like this.

When he was very young, he began to drink *tragos* [drinks, shots] — he learned to do it with bad street friends. His father, Don Gregorio, was a *zajorín* [shaman], and many people came to him in order to perform *costumbres* [rituals]. They gave him many gifts of *guaro* [firewater, sugarcane rum]. Quique also drank his *tragos* when his father was careless with the bottles. He liked to get drunk like a grown-up. But the misfortune is that he didn't want to work with a hoe in the field and he didn't have money to buy the drinks. His father became very angry when he saw him drunk, wanting to banish him from the house, but finally his father pardoned him on the condition that he had to work in the field. He says, however, that he was an enemy of fieldwork. He wanted to learn an easier job in order not to suffer so much. He thought about the work of his father, of being a *zajorín,* but he was afraid to tell him. Quique thought it better to learn to be a good *brujo* [witch] in order for it to be easier to get money and *guaro.*

One day he says that he had the opportunity to talk with a real *brujo* named Pedro Quem, and he asked him to teach him the art of being an able *brujo.* The *brujo* told him that with much pleasure he would teach him how to become a competent *brujo,* but on the condition that he withstand the tests of the *dueño* [owner, god] of the cemetery. The *brujo* said they would have to go four times to the cemetery on Wednesdays and four times on Fridays at exactly twelve midnight. After the tests, or baptism, the owner of the cemetery would give him the herb (bone of a dead person) as a power, but this would be later.

Then Wednesday arrived, and they went to the cemetery at midnight. The two entered together, but before arriving at the center, the *brujo* told Quique to stay some distance behind and to observe what he was going to do. Quique said he felt a great fear when the *brujo* said these words to him.

The real *brujo* lay down in the center of the cemetery with his face toward the ground. Quique says that at this moment there came up a big whirlwind in the middle of the cemetery. Quique, trembling with fear, didn't sense it when he fell to the ground. For a moment, he heard *habladas* [words being said, speech] but he didn't understand anything, which scared him more. He wasn't able to get up until the *brujo* came to get him up and ask him what he had heard and seen. But Quique answered that he didn't see anything except a whirlwind that came up in the center of the cemetery. He heard words but he didn't understand anything, and he couldn't see anymore because he fell to the ground, almost unconscious. The *brujo* said that Quique was afraid because it was the first time, but the next time he would be able to see something good.

The day arrived and they went again to the cemetery. Before the *brujo* entered, he gave a *trago* to the apprentice, and he gave him a little piece of a *secreto* [magical or sacred object] for encouragement. The *secreto* was a little bit of a bone of a dead person. Like this, they entered the cemetery. Quique stopped and the teacher went another time to the center and lay down with his face toward the ground. At the same time a whirlwind started, and the wind was really strong. The hardy drink that the student had taken gave him courage, and he could see that in the whirlwind a large man rose up with an ugly face and enormous teeth, grabbed the *brujo* by the neck, stood him up, and jabbed him in the ribs with a lance. He says that the *brujo* didn't shout or speak. He acted as if nothing had happened. Right away the wind calmed and the man disappeared in the same place. Then the *brujo* got up, made his way to where he had left the apprentice, and asked him if he had seen something. He said yes. Then the *brujo* told him that the next time the same thing would happen to him. The two left the cemetery and each went to his home. But Quique couldn't sleep at all; every time he wanted to close his eyes, the man with the ugly face and enormous teeth presented himself to him.

The third time the *brujo* told him that they would go to the cemetery. "Fine," said Quique, and they went at midnight. The *brujo* stayed behind, sent the apprentice to the center of the cemetery, and ordered him to assume the same position he had seen his teacher assume. Quique had a lot of fear, but he had to obey. He lay facedown, heard when the whirlwind began, and felt as if he had been given a great blow to the back or to the heart. From that instant he felt nothing, as if he were dead. Soon the *brujo* grabbed his hands and pulled him up. But Quique said that still he could barely walk to get to his house. The *brujo* told him that it would not do for him to be a *brujo;* he didn't have enough courage. Thus he said that he went to the cemetery only three times, not the five times he needed to complete his training.

Quique Miguel became sick for several days; he could not sleep at night because his soul had remained with the *dueño* of the cemetery. Since his father was a shaman, he had to perform four *costumbres* in the cemetery at night with him. His mother [who had to assist in the *costumbres*] had to keep performing certain *secretos* until he was cured.[27]

Quique says that he was a mischievous young man after he was cured of the ill he had suffered. He always had in mind that he wanted to learn something in his life. One day he managed to speak with a man who was a *characotel* [person who turns into a *nagual* and acts as a spy or does evil]. The *nagual* [animal form of a person, or spirit] of this man, he says, was a cat. Then Quique asked the man to teach him how to become a good *characotel*.

The *characotel*-man told him that to learn was easy and that he didn't want money. "The only thing that I ask of you, when you are learning, is that we will be two friends together. We will go during the nights to pursue the people who are sick because this is the work of the *characotel*."

"With much pleasure. Teach me and I will accompany you at night. We will be a pair," responded Quique.

He said that on the first night they went to the house of a person who was seriously ill and whose relatives were taking care of him. Then Quique and the *characotel* made their way to this home to pester the sick man so that he would die. They say that the house of the sick person had been emptied in order to receive visitors—all of the earthenware jars, pots, and bowls were on the porch. Then Quique and his teacher went to the porch of the neighboring house. The teacher said to Quique, "You wait here, watching. When you hear the noise of the bowls, jugs, and pots, don't move for anything. I will come to protect you. I know what I am going to do so that the relatives of the sick man don't see."

"Fine," replied Quique, but he said that he began to tremble. He felt very cold and felt his hair stand on end from pure fright. He remembered what had happened before in the cemetery. The *characotel*-man went to the porch of the sick man, put his hands and head on the ground, raised his feet, and let himself fall faceup, doing this four times. But each time that he fell, it seemed that bowls, pots, and jars were breaking.

When the relatives heard that someone was breaking the clay utensils on the porch, they went running with sticks and stones. While some said they saw a *characotel* that was a cat, others said they saw a man. They were confused. Then they went to inspect the earthenware things. But everything was fine; nothing had broken. The *characotel*-man calmly went to get the apprentice and tell him, "Now you see that this is what you do to frighten the sick, even frightening their relatives. Why don't you go now and scare someone who is sick?"

The relatives of the sick man tried to look for what was harassing them, but they didn't manage to see, even though they passed by very close. Finally, they became tired and returned to the sick man. After a while the *characotel* went again to do the same thing, but the relatives didn't manage to see anything, even though they passed by very close. Quique said they did this for three nights.

The next week the sick man continued the same way, very ill, but he hadn't died. Then the master *characotel* went to call Quique, and they went to the house of the sick man to pester him at night. The *characotel* teacher said to Quique, "I will remain on the porch of the other house while you go to do what I have taught you. If the children of the sick man come out, don't run. Come calmly where I am staying. I am your protection, but take great care not to run to the other side because then they will manage to see you."

"Very well," said Quique. He went to the hallway of the house of the sick man where the pots, bowls, jugs, and other earthenware were. This was an opportunity for him, and he put his hands and head on the ground and raised his feet upward and fell with his face upward. But since he didn't have his *nagual* like the other [*characotel*], right then all of the clay things began to break. He did it only two times. Then the sons of the sick man came out and managed to see that it was a man, and they ran to him to give him a beating.

Quique lost his composure, or—worse—he forgot what his teacher had said. When the sons of the sick man came running, Quique became frightened, and he didn't go where [the teacher] was waiting. To the contrary, he went running to the other side, and the teacher could now do nothing about the people running behind to capture Quique. Since he was young, he could run well, but because of bad luck, he crossed a row of rocks when he was running. The rocks knocked Quique down, and he stayed down, with a broken hip and knee. He was in great pain, but he could not shout because nearby passed the children of the sick man who were looking for him in order to kill him. Fortunately, they didn't see him, and they returned home.

Quique said that little by little he got up from beneath the stones but he couldn't walk. He was there the rest of the night. Not until the next day did they carry him back, but he didn't say that he had been chased because he was a *characotel*. He told them that the rocks knocked him down when he was taking care of his necessities [defecating] in the bushes.

He said that he was sick for three months. They had to cure him, and his father had to go to perform a *costumbre* in the place [that it happened] so that his soul would return. Since then he hasn't talked anymore to *characoteles* or to *brujos*. What happened caused him a lot of shame, and because of this, he had to leave his town and find work in the capital of Guatemala.

This is a true story, and the same person told it to me. He told me that the *brujos* and the *characoteles* always exist but that they are very bad because they never want anyone else to learn.

Enrique Miguel Menéndez, whose father was a *brujo*

The Oldest Tale of My Town

The old and important people tell how it was in my town, San José. It is said that in San José there was a lot, but really a lot, of wealth. When the people sowed their fields, they reaped really good harvests—abundant rice and beans. Besides, the land was completely owned by *Sanjoseños* [people of San José]; in those days the *Martineros* [people of San Martín] didn't have land in San José. In San José there were very sacred places, such as Chua Suj, Xe Cristalín, Pa Tz'alu, and Nic'aj K'im. When our ancestors lifted up the stones, they found gold, a lot of gold. That was the wealth of the pueblo. It is said that more gold was found when the people performed *costumbres* [rituals, customs] in the hills, asking the gods for goods. Then the same gods took the gold and put it on the path of the worshipers. They say it was like this for a long time. The people of San José suffered nothing then because they had gold. But they began to suffer later, after they had beaten a priest when he was performing a mass.

To this town a priest would come and celebrate the mass, but the obligation of the town was the upkeep of the priest for the days that he stayed in San José. The parish was based in San Martín; that is, the padre stayed in San José when it was his turn to celebrate the mass. But they say that this priest was bad—he eliminated many of the ancient *costumbres*. He was the worst enemy of the *zajorines* [shamans]. The people were annoyed. Most of them were angry, but since they could not speak Spanish, they could not protest the injustice they felt.

Earlier, the *Joseños* had fed the padre well—they gave him food, they gave him beef, eggs and beans, and chicken, because then there was an abundance of chickens. But after seeing the bad behavior of the padre, they looked for ways to annoy him so that he would leave the pueblo before he eliminated the native culture of the town. To encourage the priest to leave San José, they agreed not to give him chicken, beef, eggs, or beans as a punishment. But it is said that this padre didn't want to go because he had a contract with his jefes. He would leave the town but only after he had eliminated all the indigenous *costumbres*. Then the townspeople began to punish him more severely, not even giving him his tortillas, but the padre celebrated the mass like this with hunger, putting up with the punishments of the town.

The townspeople met and said that they were going to give only avocados to the padre to eat. At that time, there was an abundance of avocados. They wanted to do this in order not to spend more money on him and to get him to leave town.

Then, like this, it went. The padre, out of pure necessity during the days that
he was to be in San José, had to eat avocados instead of beef, instead of chicken,
instead of eggs and beans. He had to eat avocados three times a day, and from
eating so many avocados he got sick to his stomach with vomiting and diarrhea.
The people were very content, planning on the death of the padre, but the padre
was invincible, sick but saying the mass as he had become accustomed.

The people acted as if they were faithful, but it is certain that they looked for
ways to annoy the padre. One morning the priest began to say the mass, sick to
his stomach from eating so many avocados, having diarrhea and vomiting. While
in the middle of the mass, he farted. When the people heard the fart of the padre,
they got very angry and asked him to suspend the mass. They ran to cut branches
from the lemon trees with many thorns and began to whip the priest inside the
church, striking him very hard. The padre almost died from the thorns that
wounded his body. Because of the blows and wounds, he was sick in bed for many
days. Later, little by little, he recovered.

When the padre felt better in health, he asked for pardon from the people of
the town. He told them he had committed a sin of passing wind during the mass
but it was because he was very sick to his stomach from eating so many avocados.
He asked the favor of the people to give him permission to celebrate a last mass,
since he was leaving. With much pleasure he was retiring from San José.

The people allowed the priest to celebrate the final mass but nothing more.
They didn't notice, however, that the padre said a mass to ask for a great punishment for the entire town. When the reverend was in the middle of the mass, he
took off the sacerdotal cloth and stole, put the chasuble inside out, turned the
missal upside down on top of the altar, and cried bitterly. Ending the mass, he
took off his shoes, shook off the dirt inside the church, and put them back on.
Then he left town. The final mass was a mass of revenge, so that this town would
pay with sufferings for the evil that they had done to the padre.

After the father left, the town began to suffer. No longer able to harvest as
before, the people no longer had corn or beans. A calamitous poverty resulted
when the *Sanjoseños* began to sell their land into the hands of the *Martineros*.[28] They
began to drink too much. This is how it was. Each day, as the poverty worsened
and the people no longer could support themselves, many went to the coast to
work on the farms, no longer living in the town.

It was like this when the town lost its wealth; from then on, there was no gold
in the hills. The old folks say that the wealth of San José left the great hill,
Cristalín; it went to a place called Bocó in Santo Tomás Chichicastenango. (I
don't know if this place is called Bocó now, but they say that earlier there was
a place named Bocó, an enchanted place of great wealth where the *zajorines* and

brujos [witches] went to do *costumbres,* asking for wealth of the *dueño* [owner, god] of the Bocó Hill.)

Because of this, they say that the people of Chichicastenango and Santa Cruz del Quiché are rich owners of many goods, but the wealth was from San José. It was lost because the *Joseños* committed the most serious sin of whipping a padre when he was celebrating a mass. For that reason, the town became very poor—all of the land passed into the hands of the *Martineros.* It is said that the *Martineros* made these gains because they were very obedient to the priests. Because of this, they are very rich and the *Joseños* are very poor.

The *Joseños* had in mind that our ancestors had committed a great sin. Then in the years 1948 to 1949, a priest named Rogelio came each month to San José to celebrate mass. The parish was then based in Sololá, and when he came to say mass, he slept in the monastery of the town.

One night the *principales* [elders] and *cofrades* [members of a *cofradía*] told Father Rogelio the story of the *Joseños* of earlier times who had hit a padre. They told him that the people were paying with poverty for what the padre had done during the final mass.

Father Rogelio responded: "There is the need to ask pardon of God so that he forgives the sins that the ancestors committed, but it is necessary to celebrate four masses on Cristalín Hill, so that God lays his hand again on the town of San José." The *principales, cofrades,* and townspeople in general became very pleased with the padre.

Then the mass of the following month was not celebrated in the church. All of the ornaments were taken [out of the church], and the mass was celebrated on the Cristalín Hill. The people of the town were very pleased, and all of them went to the hill to ask God's forgiveness.

Thus it was. The padre agreed to celebrate the next mass on the same Cristalín Hill, and he returned to Sololá. This same padre also celebrated masses in the other towns of the lake.

One day Father Rogelio went to celebrate mass in San Benito la Laguna [a pseudonym]. Because of such bad *suerte* [luck], when the reverend finished the mass, a strong wind whipped up. Out of fear of traveling over the lake, the priest arranged to spend the night and leave early the next morning, because the following day he was scheduled to say mass in Sololá. In those days, it took three hours to cross the lake.

At 3:00 A.M. three *Beniteños* [people of San Benito] began rowing Father Rogelio across the lake. When they embarked, the wind was calm. As they were passing in front of Tzununá, a very strong north wind began to blow. The three boatmen were not experts at crossing the lake. Losing its balance, the canoe capsized, with everyone aboard falling in the water. That is when Father Rogelio lost his life, together with two of the rowers. Only one survived.

Many people of San Martín, San José, San Jorge [a pseudonym], and Santa Cruz tried to find the remains of the body of Father Rogelio, but they were unable. Even divers from the capital could not find them. For the *Sanjoseños* there was much sadness because it was their hope to celebrate [the next] mass on the hill, but since Father Rogelio had drowned, they could not. [Only one of the four masses needed to purge the town of its sin had been completed.] According to our fathers, we still are atoning for the sin committed by our ancestors of beating a priest when he was saying mass.

Ignacio Bizarro Ujpán

Story of the
Señor of Esquipulas
This story is very old. The old folks, people like my mother and Uncle Bonifacio, who is 83 years old and ailing, tell it.

They say that the Spaniards brought from Spain an image of a white Lord Jesús. Then all of the Cakchiqueles, Quiches, and Tzutuhiles were obligated to go worship the Holy Christ, and if they did not do it, they were executed by those same Spaniards. There were many Indians who were massacred only because they denied the existence of the Holy Christ. Many of the indigenous Maya didn't believe in the saint that the Spaniards had brought, and for this they died.

Then, the story says, the Spaniards got the idea to paint the image of Christ black to convince the Indians to abandon their gods.[29] They had to agree to idolize and adore the Holy Christ so as not to be put to death. But in order to visit and worship it, fifteen or twenty days were needed, because the place, now called Esquipulas, was far away.

It was like this when the Maya were obligated to abandon their own culture and forget their gods. The punishment they suffered was severe. If a woman didn't want to go to Esquipulas, she was tortured savagely—they cut off her breasts. For the man, the penis and the testicles were cut off as an example to the rest. So that they would quit torturing them, our fathers say that little by little they surrendered and accustomed themselves to going to visit the Holy Christ in Esquipulas. They went on foot, looking for paths in order to pass because there wasn't a road and the automobile was unknown.

It was like this when our fathers adapted to the religion of the Spaniards. Later, they say, it was no longer an obligation, but the Indians stuck to it as a custom, and they discovered many miracles in the Holy Christ. From these Tzutuhil lands the people carried those who were sick to Esquipulas, and when they returned, it is said that those who had been sick came back walking—they had been cured by miracles of the Holy Christ of Esquipulas. These same persons were witnesses that in truth the saint is miraculous, truly divine. It was like this when the majority of the Cakchiqueles, Mames, Quichés, and Tzutuhiles came to believe that Jesus Christ is truly the living son of God.

Much later, it is said, the *Sanjoseños* [people of San José] organized themselves in groups. They couldn't go with just two or three persons because it was all mountainous and they feared the coyotes and mountain lions, since wherever they were when night fell was where they slept. In this same place they gathered around a fire, cooked coffee, and ate dry *totopostes* [tortillas of coarsely ground and toasted corn] as penance in order to obtain the blessings of the Savior of Esquipulas.

But the *viejitos* [old folks] say that [the custom] is very delicate; in order not to deceive, one must do it with total faith. When one says, "I am going," or "We are going to make a trip as a pilgrimage," then one must do it with all one's heart, so as not to deceive the holy name of the Black Christ of Esquipulas. Otherwise, those persons easily die. It is said that when the soul desires a good thing and the body does not carry it out, the soul becomes sad and separates from the body. That is when people die suddenly.

It is said that once some *Joseños* agreed to go on a pilgrimage to Esquipulas to worship the Holy Christ. They formed a group and set the day that they would depart. The women began to make the *totopostes* and other food for the trip. Among them was a couple, a man named Pascual and his wife named Catarina, very desirous of knowing the Holy Christ in order to worship him. But of all the people of the town, they were the poorest. Pascual and Catarina wanted to prepare food for the pilgrimage. They wanted to ask Christ to end the poverty that they had been punished with, that they had suffered for many years. They passed by many houses, asking that they be lent corn and beans, saying that they would return them when they received a miracle from the Savior. But they didn't obtain the food. The people had contempt for them, responding that they would not be able to return the corn or beans because they were the poorest people in the town. And this is how it was. The two didn't get what they needed to make the trip.

The day arrived that the group had to go. The two poor people passionately wanted to go as pilgrims, but they could not go because they did not have provisions for the road. So Pascual and Catarina stayed. Their companions left on the pilgrimage that would take eight or ten days of traveling in one direction.

The pilgrims had been traveling for three days when Pascual and Catarina fell sick with a serious fever and died. Then their neighbors undertook responsibility for burying them because they had no relatives. In those days they didn't use boxes for burying the dead. Thus Pascual and Catarina were wrapped in *petates* [palm mats], and they were buried in their *sitio* [homesite]. There were no cemeteries.

This is how it was when they died. The people criticized the death of these two persons a lot, saying that they died because they had deceived the Holy Christ by not carrying out what they had promised. For this, they paid with their lives.[30]

The members of the group that had gone on the pilgrimage were very content without knowing what had happened in the town; that is, without knowing the fate of Pascual and Catarina. It is said that they were two days from Esquipulas when they were reminded of the two who had remained at home. Finally, they gathered at the fire to cook beans, and that night they lay down beneath the trees. All night, however, they couldn't sleep — they felt bothered, as if something had come over them. It was like this until dawn.

The pilgrims continued traveling, but they had not journeyed far when they met Pascual and Catarina returning from Esquipulas, happy with smiling faces. The group said that it puzzled them a lot because they had not yet arrived [at Esquipulas]. Pascual and Catarina spoke: "You have not yet arrived. We already are returning from visiting the *Santo Cristo de Esquipulas.*"

Then, it is said, the others answered, "How is it that you already returned? When we left, you stayed in town. It cannot be that you already are returning."

They answered:

We are the poor ones of the town to whom the people didn't want to lend corn or beans, and for this reason, it was not possible for us to come with you. But we came alone by a shortcut, and because of this, the distance was brief. Our desire to visit the Holy Christ was great; now we feel content, and we will return to our town. You need only walk a little farther to arrive there. Good-bye forever.

Then they walked a little, and they disappeared.

The others were confused because after walking a little the couple vanished. They didn't know what had happened to the couple, whether they went into the thicket or continued on the road. Well, the group of *Joseños* continued traveling. They thought that they truly had seen Pascual and Catarina. Then they arrived at Esquipulas, and they visited the Holy Christ.[31] They made their offerings as they wished.

They returned very content, mindful that they had brought a blessing from the Señor. When they arrived in the town, they were given the sad news that Pascual and his wife had died. The pilgrims were frightened, and they could not figure out what to do. They felt like fools, because they were sure they had seen these two persons; they even talked to them when they were headed to Esquipulas.

Then it was thought that they had talked to the spirits of Pascual and Catarina. They were no longer flesh and bone. Because they had wanted to visit the Holy Christ so much when they were alive but couldn't, they did so after they died, as spirits. For this reason, it is believed that when you want to do something good, you must do it with all your heart in order to not suffer the consequences. Because of this, the *viejitos* of my town have a lot of respect for the Holy Christ of Esquipulas, and they always tell this tale as an example of keeping respect for the saints.[32]

Elena Bizarro Soto and Bonifacio Soto Bizarro[33]

The Woman Who Died for Three Days and Went to Get Acquainted with Hell

A woman was the descendant of a rich family with many goods such as money, land, cattle, pigs, and chickens. The parents of this woman were extremely egotistical, envious, and miserable. They valued themselves for the riches they had and treated the poor people badly.

This is how it was when the parents of this woman died. She remained alone with her riches; that is, with the inheritance from her parents. She didn't have a husband or brothers and sisters. She didn't know what to do with the money; she wasn't able to manage the goods—a lot of land, cattle, pigs, and chickens.

So went the life of this woman. She concerned herself only with looking after her goods. The animals multiplied. Afraid that someone would steal her money, she didn't want anyone to go on her land. Always, she displayed bad character. She didn't want to have anything to do with the poor people, refusing to look at or speak to them because she was the only one who had good possessions in the town.

With the passage of the years, the woman became older each day, and she fell sick. But the citizens and the people of the town were not encouraged to visit her, because she was bad; that is, they were afraid of her.

Thus it was. The sickness was advancing, and the woman now wasn't able to walk or get up. She remained in bed. From her bed she called for someone to give her a glass of water or a little food. But it is said that the poor people were united against giving any charity to this ungrateful woman.

This woman, now very sick, thought about her large sums of money and about the documents to all her goods. Little by little, she got up at night so that no one would see her and buried the money in her *sitio* [homesite]. She did the same with the deeds to her land, burying all the papers in a big hole in the *sitio*.

Within a few days the woman died, but it was very sad because no one wanted to do her the favor of burying her. Finally, the citizens thought of giving a burial to this woman, but as they were poor, they were unable to provide the money to buy the box [coffin]. Some of them searched hard for her money because they knew that she was rich, but it was impossible for them to find it. Others tried to look for the documents to the land to see if they would be able to sell a piece of property to cover the expenses of the interment, but they could not find the papers. Finally, the citizens took up a collection for the coffin. But, it is said, the neighbors next to the house felt very preoccupied because the body of the woman was three days old and it was emitting a foul odor. At the moment of the closing of the coffin, the woman moved, sighed, and sat up. The people ran outside, scared because they knew that the woman had been dead for three days.

It is said that the woman revived and began to speak. The people, trembling with fear, now did not want to enter, but with the help of God, they caught their breath and mustered the courage to go into the house of the woman again to hear what she had to say.

The woman called the people that were there, told them not to be afraid, and began to speak:

Forgive me. I am a bad woman. Never did I want to share with the poor people. Now I indeed understand that the wealth of this world is not worth anything in the next life. My father and mother enjoyed this life and lacked nothing, but now they are tortured in hell, receiving cruel punishment from the devil, burning day and night and not a drop of water to drink. I saw my parents wallowing with the demons in the eternal fire. My life is lost. I am sure if I don't repent I will end up in the place of great suffering where my parents are.

She began to cry, and she said that she had seen another group of persons who were dressed in the color of sky blue, passing among flowers, enjoying a marvel, and singing the name of God. She wanted to take part with the group, but then a man told her that she had nothing to do with those who were dressed in sky blue. She had to go to hell, where she encountered the bad ones. This same man said that she would return to earth for some days to repent for all the evil she had done.

The woman got up from the coffin, began to walk, and told the people, "Come. Dig here. Here, I have buried the money. Divide it among yourselves." And she began to walk a little more ahead, and then she said, "Dig. Here, I have buried the documents to all the property."

The people dug as she directed them, and right there they found the money and the documents. They divided the money and land among themselves.

Then she told them, "Now that you have the money and the land, I want you to divide the cattle."

"Good," said the people, and each one got a bull.

"Good," said the woman. "Now I want you to divide the pigs."

"Good," said the people, and each one of them got two pigs.

Finally, she said:

For all that I have done to you, I hope that God will spare my soul from hell. I know that I have only a few days of life, and I ask that when I die you will bury me. All of you have a good fiesta and eat some of my chickens. Eat the rest of them nine days after my burial and direct your prayers for my soul, because I know that further beyond there is an eternal suffering, the hell where my parents are going to be forever.

God save me. Don't let me end up with them.

This is what the woman did. After being dead for three days, she came back to life to divide all the things that she had. She lived only three days more, and then she died once and for all.

Elena de Dios[34]

The Louse Who Caused the Death of the Womanizing King: A Tzutuhil Story
A king who had been governing a long time over the land was a king who liked women. He was bad but more so with the men. He handed out severe punishments, and he sent the men to war so that he could remain with the women. He was finishing off the men of the towns.

Then a certain day arrived when the men gathered and said:

What are we going to do? The king is going to finish killing us off so that our women can remain for him. It can't be that only one king will finish us off; now we have to look for our defense.

Among the people, there were many kinds of specialists such as *zajorines* [sha-mans], *brujos* [witches], and *characoteles* [people who turn into *naguales,* or animal forms of people or spirits, and act as spies or do evil]. The *zajorines* performed many *costumbres* [rituals] to torment the king, but nothing worked. The *brujos* performed many *costumbres* to persecute the king, but they didn't work either.

The *characoteles* assembled, planned many things to cause the death of the king, and carried them out. But since the king was a very strong man, for him the *zajorines, brujos,* and *characoteles* were ineffective. The men weren't able to do anything to defend themselves from the great punishments. Each day the men were being decimated, and their wives were going to the king. This king had a lot of concubines, and everywhere he had children.

Again the men who survived got together, and again they spoke of looking for a way to defend themselves from the injustices of the wicked king. They all said that the owl should be called because he was the animal that had more power than a *brujo.* They also said that the cat should be summoned because the cat was an animal who had more power than a *characotel.*[35]

First the men spoke to the owl, asking him to persecute the king. All the men offered to compensate the owl with good chickens since the owl likes to eat only chickens.

The owl said, "With much pleasure I will persecute the king, but I need to call the rest of my companions."

Then the men spoke to the cat, offering to remunerate him with mice until he was well gorged. He, too, said he would help.

Then the owls and the cats agreed to help the men. Every night the owls had to sit on the house of the king [hooting] to capture his spirit until it made him become sick.

The cats agreed to make the king sick by screeching loud meows over the loft of the house. "With this the king will be more scared and will die of fright," they said.

They carried out their plan to perform witchcraft against the king. The day arrived, and the owls began their racket—"hoot, hoot, hoot," the sound of the owls. Also the cats began their screeching on the loft of the house.

One day the king fell sick; day by day the situation got worse. The men became very content when they learned the state of the king, who was seriously ill. They awaited the day that he would die.

But as the king was resourceful, he sent for all the wise men and diviners in the whole domain of his kingdom to diagnose him—to determine why he was sick and to see if there was a cure.

Then the wise men and diviners told the king that he was being persecuted by the owls and the cats, who were contracted by his enemies. But for a solution, they told him to post soldiers during the night to control the owls and the cats. If he would do this right away, he would recover his health.

"Good," said the king, and he ordered the soldiers to go on alert with their arms.

Well, the owls and the cats arrived during the night to continue their persecution of the king, but they were able to do nothing because the soldiers discharged their weapons and many owls and cats died. Thus they were not able to help the men.

When the king recovered his health, he became even crueler with the men and with the animals. And no one could look inside his palace. He dictated double punishment for the men, and they could not complain because no other person could command the evil king.

Then one day the men agreed to give their opinions on how to resolve the problem from which they had been suffering. Some said that they didn't have any friends other than the animals of the field and the trees. Others said the owls and the cats already had not worked out. Then they decided to look for a bull because he was an expert in something good.

The men talked to a very tame bull. They expounded on the problem from which they were suffering. Although the bull was very tame, he got angry and sided with the king, saying:

The king is doing very well to punish you men three times as badly because you are without shame. You were killing and eating many of us bulls, but the king stopped you. That's the reason you will get no help from me.

Without gaining anything, the men returned discouraged.

Then they went to ask the horse for his help, but the horse was worse than the bull. Instead of giving them advice, he kicked at them and said:

The king is better than all you men, and I hope he finishes you off so that we horses will find a little peace and tranquillity. Daily we suffer, carrying heavy loads and receiving cruel punishment. You men eat the best that you find, and for us there is only a little grass. Better if you men were the horses and we were you, because we are better than you. We will not help you. Go to hell.

The few men who remained were looking for a way to defend themselves from this misery. They gathered together again to find a way to kill the king. They began to concentrate, and then one of them spoke: "Let's go to look for the rabbit because he is the most intelligent animal."

"Yes," they all said, and they left for the field to look for a rabbit to consult.

However, each time the men wanted to approach a rabbit, it ran away, because the rabbits were very afraid of the men, thinking that they would kill them.

Finally, they found a rabbit who was a little sick, lying down underneath a rock; he hardly was able to run. One of the men spoke to this rabbit, and he told him what they had been suffering for many years. The rabbit didn't respond to the man. The man told him, "Brother rabbit, we would like you to give us an idea."

The rabbit answered angrily and said, "Don't call me brother. I am not a pervert or an enemy of the king, nor do I have enemies in the world."

But finally they convinced him. Then the rabbit told them:

I am unable to do anything to help you because I am an animal of the field. I can't go into the house of the king, but look for a mouse and a louse. They can enter the house of the king, and if they succeed, the king is yours. He will die. Then you men will find peace and tranquillity. When you find a mouse and a louse, tell them to come to me, and I will tell them what to do. What they must do is difficult and delicate.

The men left in search of a mouse and a louse, but the mice were also very much afraid of the men, thinking that they wanted to kill them. At last, they found a mouse working in a patch of reeds, and this same mouse had a louse. Then one of the men spoke to the mouse:

Dear mouse, we men have been suffering a misery for a long time—the injustices of an evil king. Now, we have talked with the rabbit, and he told us to talk to you and the louse so that together you will help us. [In return for your service] we don't mind giving you part of our corn and beans; we will give you our seed, our chili. We don't mind giving the louse drops of our blood [in return for his service].

"Very well, very well, but afterward, don't be sorry," said the mouse.

But for the louse, it was difficult to walk. He had to climb on top of the mouse, and they took the road to where the rabbit was.

When they arrived, they discussed [the situation] among themselves. Then the rabbit told the mouse and the louse, "The men now need our help. It is because they are suffering."

The mouse said:

We have realized, brothers, that the men are the ones who are bad, fighting among themselves and killing one another. They are egotistical and envious.

They act worse to us animals. We are innocent. When we are hungry and want to approach them, they grab stones, sticks, or machetes. They have killed many of our comrades.

"That's true," said the louse. "Each time that we lice want to drink some drops of blood, the men squash us with their fingernails. We should not help them stop the injustices of the king."

"There is one thing," said the mouse to the louse. "I want to hear what the rabbit has to say, whether we should help them or not."

Then the rabbit spoke:

I don't need the men. I live in the field, and my food is grass. But you, indeed, need the men. You mice live off the corn, beans, chili, seeds, and other things that men grow. You lice need men because when they sleep, you feed off their blood. But if all the men die, you too are going to die. And for this not to happen, it is better that you help the men for your own existence.

The mouse and the louse were convinced.

This, then, was the advice the rabbit gave to the mouse to make the king sick:

Look for a way to get into the house of the king. Carry the louse as cargo, because he is not able to go alone. And remember, anyone can squash you at the entrance with his shoe.

"But," said the mouse, "I don't have any idea. My head doesn't help me. I don't know what to do to be able to go inside."

The rabbit told the mouse:

You have to be ready near the large door. When the servants enter, then you enter. They won't realize it. Procure your food at night so that nothing bad will happen to you. You must stay there until the louse does his work well.

Then the rabbit told the louse:

When you enter the bedroom of the king, check things out well. When he is fast asleep, bite him on the most delicate parts of his body. But do it with much care, because when the king feels the bites, he will begin to scratch. Bite him in such a manner that he can't grab you with his nails.

Then the louse asked, "What part of the body is very weak? Is it the nose or the ears?"

The rabbit answered:

No, you need to bite him on the *culo* (ass) and on the end of his *pipe* (penis), but with much precaution. First bite him on the *culo;* then, when the king begins to scratch his *culo,* bite him on the end of his *pipe.* When the king begins to scratch his *pipe,* change your position. But do it with much care. Don't allow him to grab you with his nails because it will be you who will die first. The same king will hurt his own body from so much scratching of his *culo* and *pipe.* It is certain that the bites will become infected. Continue biting him until he becomes seriously ill. The king, when he feels gravely ill, will call the wise men and diviners to investigate what he is suffering from and whether the illness has a cure. But take care when the wise men and diviners arrive at the house of the king. They will be able to do nothing; they will only say the king has a malignant, incurable disease.

Then the king will send for the best doctors in the world, but they will be able to do nothing. You continue biting and making him suffer in accordance with all that he has done to the men. But you have to be very clever when the best doctors of the world arrive. They will take off his clothing to examine him. You must hide in the hairy part of his body so that the doctors will not see you with their apparatus (equipment). I know that the doctors can't take care of what I'm telling you to do.

"Good," said the mouse and the louse, and they left to do the job. They managed to enter the house of the king. Without wasting time, the louse began to bite the king on his most delicate parts.

The king felt irritated on his *culo* and *pipe.* He began to scratch and scratch until an infection developed on his bottom and on his male member. But the king did not know that it was the louse that was biting him. He knew that his room was very clean.

This is the way it went every night. He was bitten, and a lot of scratching caused his rump and male organs to become infected.

He called the wise men and diviners, but they did nothing to cure him. Seeing the seriousness of the affliction, the king called the best doctor so that he would heal the sickness. But the science of medicine failed, and the sickness of the king persisted. He now could not urinate or defecate. Each day he grew worse until he died of the infection caused by the louse.

When the king died, the louse got on top of the mouse, and they went to where the rabbit was to tell him that the job was completed. Not until then did the men experience more tranquillity. For the work they did to free the men from the injustice of the wicked king, the rabbit [now] has the right to eat their vegetables; the mouse has the right to eat their corn, beans, chili, seeds, and other things that men grow; and the louse has the right to suck drops of their blood.

Ignacio Bizarro Ujpán[36]

Story of an Enchanted Place, Paruchi Abaj

This story of the hunters and the haunted rock is very old.[37] Our ancestors told it, but these days only a few still tell it. It is believed that in this enchanted place, Paruchi Abaj, the *dueño* [owner, lord, master] comes out every twenty days at midnight sharp. People wanting to become rich in this life and hunters wanting to kill game go to him to make offerings.

They say that the *dueño* of the place is a man with red skin, red all over his body. When the time arrives for the *dueño* to come out, the rock begins to thunder, making as if it were a big earthquake, and the stone opens like a door. From there, out comes the enchanted man, *dueño* of Paruchi Abaj.

The people presenting the offerings have to withdraw a little because at this point it is delicate. Paruchi Abaj doesn't want them to see him.

After he receives the offerings, the rock begins to thunder again. It is the signal that it will close again. Then those presenting offerings draw near to finish the *costumbre* [ritual] that they have started, but now without their gifts. The *dueño* carries these offerings to the bottom of the cave.

Paruchi Abaj lets a hunter know whether he is pleased with his *costumbre* by appearing to him in his dream. If the enchanted one likes the gifts, he tells the hunter he has permission to hunt.

In the past it was mainly hunters who went a lot to this place to perform the *costumbres* to ask for permission to hunt. In exchange, they had to offer good presents to the *dueño* of the charmed place. They carried roosters and sheep (good and fat), or, if they didn't have roosters or sheep, they carried boneless beef. They had to be in the haunted place at midnight, the hour when the *dueño* came out from the place to receive the gifts.

In this way the hunters went to hunt animals such as deer, mountain lions, raccoons, pacas, armadillos, and wild pigs. It is said that the hunters received in their sleep the orders of the *dueño* of the animals. They had to leave the bones of the dead animals at Paruchi Abaj so that the *dueño* could control the number of animals hunted by the persons who had his permission.[38]

Then the hunters with much respect cared for the bones of the deer and other animals. Since they needed to be returned to the enchanted place, the hunters didn't leave them out. Otherwise, the hounds would eat them. When the day arrived, the hunters carried the bones and bunched them together beneath the stone of Paruchi Abaj, but they had to be guided by a *zajorín* [shaman] to present to him the *costumbre* of gratitude. They carried a lot of candles, incense, myrrh, *aguardiente* [cane liquor], and *chicha* [corn liquor, home brew].

It is said that if the hunters did not ask for permission to hunt the animals, they would have bad luck. There have been times when the hunters' dogs have been lost forever, and there have been times when the hunters have been lost once and for all. If lucky, they have appeared three to five days later, but in a place different from where they had been lost.

One time a man of San José went with his dogs to hunt deer on a day when it was drizzling. Without doubt, this man did not have the permission of the *dueño* of the enchanted place, and he had bitter luck. In the afternoon of this day, only the dogs came home. The man did not come home with them. The family, it is said, went crazy looking for the hunter, but they were unable to find him.

The man appeared, but later, and this same man came to tell the people what had happened to him. He said that on the day when it was drizzling he was chasing a deer. The dogs ran ahead, yapping and trying to catch up with it. Suddenly, he no longer heard the yaps of the hounds.

He then sensed he was in an immense place where he saw many fat men and fat dogs. But he was unable to walk backward or forward. Suddenly, he recognized an uncle who had been dead for years who also had been a hunter. The uncle said:

Hello, nephew, what are you doing here? This is a place of endless suffering. They fatten us and kill us. Our flesh serves as food for the *dueños* of the hills and enchanted places, and our bones return to join together and be reincarnated again. We are like this all the time, a suffering that does not end. When I was alive, I liked to hunt to feed my family meat of the animals, but now I am paying with my life.

Nephew, my blood feeds the vampires (bats) that are the messengers of the master and lord of this place. Both the *dueños* of the enchanted hills and the *dueños* of the unenchanted hills come here to eat. The *dueño* of this place is the jefe of them. Moreover, here is the place of Nima Sotz' (the big bat) and Alaj Tak' Sotz' (the small bats), and the place of Nima Tucur (the big owl) and Alaj Tak' Tucur (the small owls). The small bats and small owls are the *alguaciles* [runners or aides], guards, commissaries, and controllers for Nima Sotz', the big bat, jefe of the small bats, and for Nima Tucur, the big owl, jefe of the small owls. The small bats and small owls have the responsibility of controlling the number of people who get sick, die, and come to this place of suffering. These are the hunters who take game without permission and the people who get their wealth from this place, both them and their families. The bats and the owls tell Nima Sotz' and Nima Tucur how many people in each town are going to come to this place.

Here come not only the hunters but also the rich who in life took their fortune from this place. In life they had a lot of luck—land, livestock, money, and many other things—but they didn't value the poor people. The poor people, however, don't come here.

Nima Sotz', the big bat, doesn't leave; he only waits on the small bats. Nima Tucur, the big owl, doesn't go out. He only waits on the smaller owls. All of them, the big and small bats, and the big and small owls, feed on our blood.

The small bats and small owls have fixed hours for leaving and returning. The two jefes give the orders when to leave and when to return. Moreover, Nima Sotz' doesn't let the bats that arrive late suck blood. He takes them outside to see where they will get their food. It is like this when the bats leave for the fields and pastures to suck blood of the livestock and horses.

It is the same with Nima Tucur; he throws outside the owls who arrive late to see how they will feed themselves. Bats have sharp points on their beaks and easily prick livestock and horses. Owls have soft beaks and mainly look for small birds, doves, and chickens because they have soft skin.

Nephew, this is all that I am telling you. It is not time for you to be here. Right now the *dueño* of this place is going to offer you food, silver, and gold, but be careful not to accept it. If you do, you will remain here once and for all. If you take the gold and silver, the *dueño* of this place will allow you to leave so that you can enjoy the riches of the world, but when you die, you and your family will all come here to this hell, a suffering that never ends. Your blood and that of your family will be for Nima Sotz' and Nima Tucur. Your flesh and that of your family will be food for the *dueños* of the hills, and your bones will be reincarnated.

The story goes that at this instant the *dueño* of the enchanted place, Paruchi Abaj, then talked to the hunter man, saying, "Here you are. Come in and eat something!"

The man answered, "No, many thanks, I'm not hungry."

The *dueño* of the place told him, "That's okay if you don't want to eat. Now I will give you this piece of gold and this piece of silver as a memento so that some day you will remember me."

The hunter answered, "No, many thanks, I don't want either gold or silver. The only thing that I have is this." And he showed him a cross that hung around his neck.

Then the enchanted one became very angry. He grabbed the man by the hair and gave him a number of kicks in the butt until he became unconscious.

The story goes that the man appeared five days after he had disappeared. He appeared in a small brook of the Camibal (river of death).[39] The man said that he felt he was in a small brook but that he felt a great fear of going to his house because he was wet, had mud on his face, and trembled from a great cold. But the people continued looking for him. Finally, they were able to find him in this small river, but not until five days [had passed]. Then they carried him to his house, where he related all that had happened to him.

This is one of the oldest tales of my town. When I was a boy, I was able to see the bones of the deer. Paruchi Abaj is very near the town.

Gerardo Bizarro Ramos and Bonifacio Soto[40]

The Story of the Assistants Who Worked with the Germans

This is the story of the arrival of electricity in Guatemala. It is said that the Germans brought the electric generators over here to Guatemala. The business of electricity was the best of all, and the money that they made they sent to Germany.

When Guatemala was growing (developing), more electricity was needed for the people, but the Germans then were not able to do much work because there were only a few of them. They came up with the idea of looking for more helpers. The helpers, pure Indians, were from Nahualá, and they began to work on Santa María Hill through Quezaltenango. They installed big electric generators operated by the [water of the] Samalá River, and thus in time the installation of electric lights was extended to the cities and towns.

Thus, when the Germans and their helpers were too few to do a lot of work, it was necessary to look for more personnel. One day, it is said, the German jefe of the helpers from Nahualá declared, "*Muchá* [muchachos], we need more heads to continue working." The jefe was referring to needing more personnel and helpers. The helpers of Nahualá, however, understood that the electric generators needed more heads of people to continue working, and the jefe told them again, "*Muchá*, we need more heads. Go get more, and I will pay you well."

"Very well, jefe," said the *Nahualeños* [people of Nahualá] and they grabbed their machetes and their sacks and took off toward Nahualá, their town. And it is said that during the night they began to cut off the heads of people, including men, women, and children. They decapitated them! On this same night they returned to the Germans, each one with his sack of heads.

"Mission completed, jefe. Here are the heads," they said.

"And where are the helpers?" asked the jefe.

"What helpers? You asked for heads, and we brought heads in the sacks," they said.

The jefe became scared and didn't know what to do with so many decapitated heads.

And that was the origin of what the people said—that for electricity they needed human heads, or bodies—but it was not true. It was just a confusion between the jefe and his helpers. But the people still believe that the electric generators need to consume human heads, or bodies. For that reason, there is a lot of fear of walking during the night.

Valeriano Temó[41]

Simple

Simón
There was a certain Simón who wanted to do something good, but because of bad luck, everything he did turned out wrong. On one occasion he was lucky. His matrimonial godfather gave him two pairs of *caites* [open-toed sandals] of the same color. Simón was very content. In all his life he had never had the opportunity to wear a pair of *caites.*

After receiving them, he went to the river with his wife to have a swim and then put on his new sandals. But when he tried to put on the sandals, they did not fit, and he became sad.

His wife asked him, "Simón, what is wrong with you?" And he answered, "It's that the *caites* do not fit well." But his wife discovered that the two *caites* were for the same foot, and she said, "Idiot, the two *caites* are for the same foot."

Simón answered, "My beloved wife, but they're just like the pair that I left at the house."

Another time, Simón passed by the shore of a lake where the people were joyful, some swimming, others fishing. Simón paused, looking at his reflection in the lake. Well, he was very content and brought back some sand in a sack, thinking perhaps he could do something similar.

Very happily he returned to his pueblo. On the road he was saying to himself, "The beach on the lake that I just passed was very pleasant; many people were swimming, some fished, while others relaxed on the sand. Why can't I do the same, I say?"

When he arrived at his house, he told his wife and his son the good things he had seen. Then Simón began to carry water from the well and put it inside a *tinaco* [large, thick clay vat]. When the *tinaco* was full, Simón scattered sand around it, forming something similar to the beach. Then he hooked a fishing line to a cane pole and sat on the patio of his house to fish.

Hours passed, and there was nothing. He began to sweat because the sun was shining intensely. Then his wife arrived and said, "Simón, what are you doing? Why are you sitting under the hot sun, sweating a lot?"

And he answered, "My beloved wife, when I went on my journey, I passed by the shore of a lake. I saw many happy people swimming and fishing, and many were on the sand. Then what I did was to bring back with me a little sand inside a sack. What you see here is the beach, and the water inside this *tinaco* is the lake. I am the fisherman, but because of bad luck, I have not caught anything."

His wife told him, "You aren't a person with bad luck; you're just a simple Simón, because only simpletons do such things." Then his wife went into the kitchen.

Simón, seeing that he was not catching any fish, took off his clothes and got into the vat in order to bathe, pretending he was in a lake.

Then his wife came out again and said, "Simón, what are you doing?"

And Simón answered, "I am inside the lake having a good swim, just like those people I saw at the lake."

His wife told him, "Simón, you are a fool. You are not in a lake but rather in a *tinaco*."

Simón, however, did not pay any attention to her. His wife went back inside the house, but she was upset because her husband was turning into a dimwit. Simón very calmly got out of the *tinaco* and lay down on the sand he had scattered around it. Then his wife came out and said, "Simón, what is happening to you? Are you loco? You are lying down on the patio of the house?"

Then he answered, "Don't you see that I just finished swimming in the lake? Now I am lying down on the sand like those people that I saw at the shore of the lake."

"You are a blockhead, Simón. How can you believe that you are on the beach when you are on the patio of the house? From now through the rest of your life, you will be called simple Simón."

Ignacio Bizarro Ujpán

Story of the Dog
and the Cat
When God, the creator, began to create all the animals, he put them in a big garden. How beautiful it was that the big animals and the small ones roamed together below the trees of the garden.

One afternoon God, the creator of the animals, began to walk in the garden among his creatures. The animals drew near to pay reverence to him, but as they were not able to speak, they shook their heads and tails, expressing to him many thanks for their lives and saying, "You are our creator."

The creator became very content with the animals, seeing the greeting that he was receiving, and said, "Grow, multiply more, and then leave the garden."

The next day the animals grew and multiplied four times more, and the garden was too small for them.

One day the creator went to stroll in the garden, thinking that he would receive more reverence, but all was to the contrary. The animals felt angry because the garden was not big enough for them. When the creator walked in the garden, they nearly ate him. Then he became full of wrath and banished them from the garden.

First he said: "Jaguars, mountain lions, and bears, [go] to the barrancas and eat what you can find." For that reason, the jaguar, mountain lion, and bear feed on the small animals.

Then he said: "Wolves and coyotes, look for your caves and endure hunger." For that reason, the coyotes and wolves now only once in a while find their food.

And the creator, still angry, said: "Deer, wild pigs, pacas, and raccoons, [go] to the banks of the rivers." And now they feed on reeds and grass.

In accordance with the creator, or God of the animals, who said these things, the animals left the garden.

Then the almighty said: "Snakes, *taltuzas* [rodents similar to rats who live under the ground], and opossums, get out of the garden and get into the holes of the earth." And for that reason, now these animals live in the holes of the earth.

Then he told the animals that had wings: "All of you, fly and make your nests in the trees and feed on what grain you can collect on the land."

Well, all the birds left flying, but the chickens, the turkeys, and the ducks could not fly much because they had finished eating and had heavy bodies. For that reason, the chickens, turkeys, and ducks aren't able to fly; they fall to the ground.

But there is one thing: when the creator was giving orders to the animals, the dog and cat hid across from where the creator was sitting. Later he realized that the dog and cat were there, and he said to them: "Stay here. Dog, you will feed on the crumbs from my cake and the rest of my food. Cat, you will feed on the mice you find in the house, and you [also] have rights to my crumbs and the rest of my food."

One day the creator left to take a walk through the garden, but he forgot to protect the cake that had been left on the table. Well, the cat and dog ate the cake.

When the master and lord returned, seeing that now there was no cake, he very angrily began to hit the dog. From so many blows the poor animal's rump was broken, and for that reason, now when the dog pees, he has to support himself on only one paw. When the creator was hitting the dog, the cat fled. For that reason, they say the cat is very much a thief and very clever.

The supreme being was very angry with the animals, and he thought it better to take them from where they were living. He gave the blessing to the dog, saying, "Go and look for your owner among the strongest beings (creatures). You have to guard him; you have to sleep with one eye closed and the other open. During the nights, you have to be vigilant so that no thieves will enter. If your owner leaves, you have to go with him. When your owner sleeps, you have to guard him."

The poor dog left the presence of the creator with his ears down and his tail between his legs. He began to walk in the mountains, barking with a voice most sad because he did not find his owner. Finally, he met the jaguar and said, "You must be the one who is most powerful."

"Of course, don't you see my robust body? There is no other animal like me," said the jaguar.

The dog said, "You are my owner; I will stay here with you."

During the night the jaguar remained seated on the hollow of a trunk, and the dog slept with the ends of his ears up, with one eye closed and the other open, as he had been told by his creator.

During the night some wild piglets came, and the jaguar was waiting to eat them. But then the dog got up and began to bark. The wild piglets were frightened and ran for the other side, and the jaguar didn't get his food.

The jaguar got mad and began to scold the dog, saying, "You are a devil. With your yaps you scared the wild piglets, and now I am left with hunger. Go to hell. You are an enemy."

The poor dog continued walking, very discouraged, without finding who would be his owner. Finally, he found a man, and he made signs by moving his tail and head, and the man caressed the dog a lot and carried him to his house. For that reason, the dog now guards the house, goes with his owner when he goes to work, and always sleeps with one eye open and the other closed.

Ignacio Bizarro Ujpán[42]

The Story of
the Tecolote

In a town lived an Indian couple. Their life was not happy but bitter and sad because their children died before they were grown. Later, a little boy was born to them. Very happily they performed *costumbres* [ritual acts] and ceremonies of birth.

Then a neighbor told them, "Now that you already have a small boy, you should get him baptized in the Catholic church, but for that you need to look for godparents who are Ladinos. The Ladinos have money and could help the boy [if sick] with some medicine so that he would not die."

"Very well," said the parents.

But since no Ladinos lived in their town, they went looking for them in other towns, passing through many towns until arriving on the coast. There they found the house of some Ladinos, but unfortunately, the father of the boy could not speak Castilian [Spanish], and neither could the Ladinos speak the Mayan language. They began to speak, but they couldn't understand one another. The best they could do was to mimic and speak by means of signs.

Finally, they accomplished the baptism with the parents and godparents very content. The parents of the baby returned to their town very happy.

But a period of bad luck came. The baby died, and again they remained alone, nothing for them.

Over time, the señora fell sick and also died. The husband remained in solitude, nothing for him. He thought it would be better to abandon his house and town for a period of time in order to learn to speak some words in Castilian. He then went to the coast to the house of the *compadres* [co-parents, godparents to the son] in order to search for a little comfort, to forget a little the bitterness of his life. He left with all his things, and when he arrived on the coast, he told his *compadres* what had happened.

The *compadres* sympathized with him and said he could stay in their house, cleaning it, preparing food, and washing clothes. Well, the single [Indian] *compadre* stayed in the house of his *compadres,* but always with a lot of pain. Since he didn't understand Spanish, he could only say *sí* and *no.*

The woman *comadre* [co-mother, godmother] was very attractive. That is, she had a full, well-proportioned body that at times captivated his attention, and every once in a while he looked at the body of the *comadre,* forgot about cleaning, and began to cry, since he found himself alone.

One day the husband and wife (the *compadres*) went to the market to buy groceries, and as something extra, they bought a *tecolote* [owl]. They put it in the window of the house, and in the nights it went, "Ju, ju, ju, ju, ju, ju." This caused a great fright for the unfortunate [Indian] *compadre*. In the nights he no longer could sleep for the fear of the *tecolote*. The *compadre* was in great despair.[43]

At dawn, the [Indian] *compadre* arrived at the kitchen for breakfast, as did the *comadre*, who said, "Compadre, how are you this morning? Did you sleep well?"

The *compadre* answered, "Ay, *comadre*, keep it quiet! I couldn't sleep well; I was afraid of *tu culote* [your butt]."

The *comadre* felt ashamed when the *compadre* said he felt afraid because of *tu culote;* she thought that he was referring to her great body, but he was really talking about the *tecolote*.

So it went every morning when the *comadre* got up. The *comadre* said, "Did you sleep peacefully?"

"Ay, *comadre,* I hardly slept for *tu culote!*" But the truth is that he meant to say "*tecolote*."

The *comadre* understood it as something else, and she said, "*Compadre,* don't be abusive. You are paying attention only to my body."

And the *compadre* answered, "It isn't that. It's that *tu culote* doesn't allow me sleep."

One day the *comadre* said to her husband, "The *compadre* is a rogue and is abusive. Every morning I ask him if he slept well, and he answers me, 'I haven't slept at all because of *tu culote*.' I feel embarrassed to give him his food. Each time he tells me '*tu culote*.' It would be better if we threw him out of the house. I don't want him to make fun of me."

The husband told her, "Let's be patient. The *compadre* doesn't have kin he can go to if we throw him out of the house."

And the *comadre* said to her husband, "Well, the *compadre* can be with us in our house, but please tell him not to say '*tu culote*.' I feel embarrassed that the *compadre* makes fun of my *culote.*"

The single [Indian] *compadre* [although he couldn't speak Spanish] understood that the *compadres* [husband and wife] were speaking badly of him. He said, "It would be better for me to go before my *compadres* kill me," and he looked for a pretext to say good-bye.

"Good-bye, *compadre,* and good-bye, *comadre.* Now I'm going to leave. By day I work, and at night I'm not able to sleep. I'm very much afraid of it. *Tu culote* is not going to make me die of fear," and he left.

Ignacio Bizarro Ujpán

Story of the Black God, Dueño of the Night

In a town lived a very poor young man. Although his parents had many goods, they viewed their unfortunate son with scorn. The parents of this boy were misers, and they didn't think that this life would end. Every day they enriched themselves, but never did they think of giving a little to their son. The unfortunate youth saw the necessity of leaving his parents because they treated him like a stranger. He left very sadly, thinking about his bad fortune.

One day when he was walking, he met a man without knowing he was the devil. And the man said to the muchacho, "What's the matter? Where are you going?"

The young man replied, "To look for work, but I don't know where. My parents treat me very badly. They don't want to give me a little of what they have. I don't have a profession; I can only make firewood," said the youth.

The devil, who had transformed himself into a man, said to the boy, "Quit being sad! I will help you with whatever you want. Go steal! There, in that house, there is a lot of money, and you can take whatever you wish to improve your life."

The young man answered, "No, señor, I don't want to steal; I'm not going to do what the devil will win my soul with," without knowing that it was with the devil he was talking. "If I were a thief, I would have stolen [things] in my parents' house, where there is a lot of money." The devil got angry at seeing he was achieving nothing with the boy.

The youngster continued on his way. Wherever he was when night fell was where he slept. He meditated and asked the god of the night to help him. The muchacho understood that there was a *dueño* (god) of night. At sunrise he continued on his way, sad and pensive.

Changing into a human form again, the devil took the shape of a beautiful woman and appeared to the muchacho. The devil, transformed into a woman, said, "Young man, where are you going? I see that you are sad and bitter with life."

The youngster answered, "To look for work; I don't know where. My parents did not want me in their house, nor did they want to give me my inheritance. What I don't have is a profession; all I can do is make firewood."

The devil, transformed into a woman, said, "An occupation doesn't matter. The only thing I ask is for you to like me, to love me, to adore me. I will make you rich. I will give you money. I will give you all the pleasures of this world."

The youth answered, "I don't want to have a woman. I don't have an occupation or money. You offer me your love, money, and pleasures. Couldn't it be that you will deliver me to the devil?"

The woman replied, "If you don't want money or pleasures, allow me to embrace and kiss you a little." In doing so, she intended to win his heart.

The young man said, "No, thanks, I don't indulge in this vice. I am traveling in search of work, to see where I can find a job as a woodcutter."

He continued walking until night fell, and he remained sleeping under some trees. But before sleeping, he had to entrust himself to the god, *dueño* of the night, so that nothing would happen to him during the night.

The next day he continued traveling. The devil transformed himself into money. When the boy continued walking, suddenly he encountered a pouch of money that was in the middle of the road. There were new bills that almost spoke, so that the man would pick them up without knowing it was the devil.

The man stopped beside the pouch, trying to decide whether to pick it up. At last he decided and said, "If I pick up this money, it could be that they will arrest me, or thieves may kill me. Lost money is like stolen money. It could be of evil; I'm not going to let the devil win me." And he continued on his way.

The angry devil could not win the soul of the youngster. He said, "I'll continue until finishing him; I will drown him in a river."

Night was falling. The boy stayed sleeping on the bank of a river, but beforehand, he had to request the protection of the black god, *dueño* of the night. When he was sleeping, a man of very small stature, his body the color black like the color of night, presented himself to the boy and said:

Muchacho, you cry and suffer in your solitude in search of work. I am the black god, *dueño* of the night, with whom you always confer and from whom you request protection. Now I want to speak to you. I will protect and look after you during the nights, but only in the nights do I have power over things. By day I see things [happening], but I cannot help. Be careful! The devil wants to win your body and soul. The man who wanted you to rob a house is the devil. The owners in that house would have killed you, and then the devil would have taken advantage of your blood.

The second time, when a beautiful woman offered you her love, it was the same devil. He wanted to take advantage of you so that you would lose your life, partaking of women and of the pleasures of this world. The third time, when on the road you encountered a full pouch of money, it was the same devil who had transformed himself into money. If you had picked up that money, you would have lost your life to avarice and drunkenness. Then the devil would have won your body and soul. Take care. The devil will continue beseeching you by day.

The youngster opened his eyes, hearing the words of the black god, *dueño* of the night. The muchacho sat down in order to answer, but at that instant he no longer saw the black god. He only heard a voice that said, "Until tonight. I'm always with you."

The next day the boy got up and continued on his way, thinking about what the black god, *dueño* of the night, had said. When the young man was crossing a river, the devil transformed himself into air, and in the river a great whirl came that flushed the unfortunate boy from one side to the other in order to finally finish him off. Accordingly, the devil thought that he had eliminated the boy. But again the boy had a lot of luck; he was able to grab a root of a tree and save his life. On the bank of this river he remained seated, crying and thinking of the bitterness of his life. Then night fell again, and he stayed sleeping within a banana plantation, always conferring with and requesting protection from the black god, *dueño* of the night.

When he was falling asleep, the man of small stature whose color was black appeared again and said:

Muchacho, I understand the sadness of your soul. The devil wants to kill you because you didn't take advantage of his offerings. Now be careful. I am always with you. By day I will help you some, but at night is when I am all-powerful. Now I tell you that the whirl of wind that dragged you in the river was the same devil transformed into air, but I put in your hand the root of a tree. With that you saved your life.

"Thank you, señor," replied the boy. "I realize that you're the black god, *dueño* of the night. I ask that you protect and help me in my solitude."

And the black god, *dueño* of the night, said to the young man, "Muchacho, the devil will always pursue you, but I will free you, providing you don't forget me."

The next day the boy continued on his journey, walking and walking until reaching the town where he wanted to work. Unfortunately, in that town, two men had quarreled to the point of coming to blows with machetes, and they died. But the people thought that some criminal had killed them, and the military commissioner and policemen were looking for the murderer.

In that town the poor young man was walking around, asking for work as a lumberjack. Again the devil transformed himself, taking the form of an old man, and he gave false testimony, telling the police that it was the young man who had killed the two men.

"Fine," said the policemen, and they took the unfortunate youth to the jail. The devil was very happy with everything that he had done.

The poor young man was crying in the jail because he had a clear conscience. He was sad because nobody was doing anything for his freedom.

When night came, before falling asleep, he entrusted himself to the black god, *dueño* of the night, requesting protection and aid while he was sleeping in the jail. In the jail the black god, taking the form of a man of small stature, appeared, rousing the youth and saying, "Wake up, young man! What's happening?" At once the boy woke up. At his side was the one who was talking to him.

The young man answered, "Here I am imprisoned without having committed a crime. An old man gave false testimony against me."

The black god, *dueño* of the night, said, "It is not a man. It is the devil taking the appearance of a man who accused you, but I will help you right now."

Then the black god, *dueño* of the night, took the boy's hand, and they peacefully left the jail [by miraculously walking through the cell door]. They were already out when the boy was struck with much pain and fear because he was afraid they could recapture him.

The black god of the night said to the boy, "Young man, don't worry. The authorities will never recapture you. I'll give you a little of my color." And he put his hands on the face and all over the body of the muchacho. At daylight the young man was a black man. The authorities had passed by searching for the fugitive, but they never recognized him. His color had been changed to black, and the devil could not recognize him either.

These were the miracles of the black god, *dueño* of the night.

Now, I have a good pony. To him who tells me another story, I will give my pony.[44]

Ignacio Bizarro Ujpán

Story of
Maximón This story is purely Tzutuhil.

It says that if Maximón wants to, he can indeed have a son with the women that he likes, but the truth is that it is not Maximón who goes to the houses of the women.[45] The women are the ones who go to the *cofradía* [religious brotherhood] of Santa Cruz.

Maximón doesn't have sexual relationships with the women. The women arrive at the *cofradía* to perform the *costumbres* [ritual acts]. In doing this, they rock the head and caress the face of Maximón. They say that at that moment the women capture his figure, but it is like the form that is in the *cofradía*. The figure that is in the *cofradía* is not as good as the real form of Maximón, which has a fine appearance and white color, as are the sons who are born by the women. These sons are *zajorines* [shamans], *brujos* [witches], and *characoteles* [people similar to witches] of great power; they do strange things.

At night they go out to drink with Maximón, their father. They say he drinks only with his real sons. Many of the *zajorines* are said to be legitimate children of Maximón, but it is a lie. They cannot do the same things his real children do.

The story says that earlier there existed two legitimate children of Maximón. One was called Francisco Sojuel and the other Francisco Ajuchan. They were of Santiago Atitlán and were of almost equal age. The people held much respect and affection for them.

They competed with the rest of the *zajorines* of the town in order to test their power, and those two came out winning. They had a meeting in the cemetery. Each *ajkum* [shaman] had to carry three *tecomates* [gourds] of *cusha* [rum moonshine], and they exchanged the *tecomates* of liquor [with one another] so that nobody could say that there was only water inside. In the meeting they began to drink and drink. The other *zajorines* with one *tecomate* of *cusha* were rolling about on the floor. But Chico [short for Francisco] Sojuel and Chico Ajuchan finished the three *tecomates* of *aguardiente* [sugarcane liquor], and they remained unfazed, as if they hadn't drunk anything.

In this meeting, they say that Maximón arrived to drink his three *tecomates* of *cusha*. Don Pedro [Maximón] and his two children laughed at the other *ajkumes* who were rolling about on the floor. There it was observed that the others were not legitimate sons of Maximón, and for spite [the two Franciscos] left them sleeping on the floor. They didn't come to their senses until the afternoon of the next day.

In another competition, they met in the nights; each *brujo* had to fix three rows of stones one meter wide. Francisco Sojuel and Francisco Ajuchan challenged the other *zajorines* to try to undo the three rows of stones with just one kick, but the other *zajorines* were unable. Chico Sojuel, with only one kick, managed to demolish the three rows of stones, and so did Chico Ajuchan. The others could only observe.

Also in that competition arrived Maximón, who also managed to demolish the three rows of stones. The other *zajorines* asked who the third [person] was, and Chico Sojuel and Chico Ajuchan responded, "It is Don Pedro, our father, and for that reason no one beats us."

And they gathered again in the nights in order to see who among them was the best. Each *ajkum* had to put together three little volcanoes [piles] of earth, each a heap of some 5 *quintales* [measures of weight of 100 pounds each]. The test was to convert the heaps of earth into dust with a single blow. The rest of the *zajorines* tried their luck, but they couldn't do anything. For the Franciscos, however, it was easy. With a single blow, they made powder of the three heaps of earth. Finally, the story says that Maximón arrived to do the same thing. The other *ajkumes* were surprised.

A final competition, the story says, is that the two Franciscos met on a shore of the lake, always in the nights, together with the other *zajorines* of the town. Everyone with his own *nagual* [spiritual or animal form] had to cross the lake to go bring fruits from the other side of the lake.[46] The rest of the *zajorines* disappeared because they were not able to cross the lake. Only the two Franciscos were able to do it. The rest who weren't able to do it had to receive a punishment of fifty lashes given by Don Pedro.

Thus, in those days, the two Franciscos were very famous. Nobody could beat them—they were the real fathers of the *zajorines* [the true sons of Maximón].

Ignacio Bizarro Ujpán

The Legend of Francisco Sojuel: A Tzutuhil Story

In the past, an Indian named Francisco Sojuel lived in Santiago Atitlán. Sojuel acted like a priest. He had spiritual powers, and, moreover, he had thirteen *naguales* [spiritual or animal forms]. Also, the story says, he was admired at one place or another for a great mental power that he had possessed since birth. He was a unique *Atiteco* [man of Santiago Atitlán]. It was certain that there were *zajorines* [shamans], *brujos* [witches], and *characoteles* [persons who can turn into *naguales* and do evil] who wanted to pester him, but they were unable. They didn't have the power that Francisco Sojuel had.

Francisco Sojuel, it is said, spoke with the saints at night when he was sleeping—that is, by means of dreams. In dreams he spoke with Santiago, San Martín, San Jacobo, and, moreover, with San Simón (Maximón). He also spoke with the *dueño del santo mundo* [owner, god of the sacred world, earth].

Once, he received an order from heaven and the *santo mundo* that he had to be the strongest person in the whole town. By means of the dream, they told him how long summer lasted and on what dates the first rains of the year would fall so that the people would not lose their first crops. Also, he received warning as to what month the illnesses would fall on the town, and he knew how many people had to die in a year.

Then it is said that in his dreams he spoke with the God of heaven and the *dueño del santo mundo,* and they told him that the town of Santiago [Atitlán] would have to suffer a great calamity of hunger for two years, that the harvests would have to go from bad to worse for lack of rain. They told him to warn the whole town to repent from their wickedness and to reserve corn, beans, and other foods so that when the punishment fell they would not have to suffer a lot.

So it was. Francisco Sojuel guided his people and told them to get closer to God and to quit doing bad things because a punishment was near that would last for two years. The whole town would have to suffer hunger and sickness; moreover, he told them to take care of the corn and beans and to save the little money that they had because the punishment would come very soon and would last for two years.

The other *zajorines, brujos,* and *characoteles* and the rest of the people treated Francisco Sojuel as a crazy man and a drunkard. They didn't believe him because he was just a man like them. Many of the people of the town paid no attention to his advice. They acted as if they had not heard anything and continued their wickedness.

But, it is said, Francisco Sojuel continued offering *costumbres* [ritual acts] to the God of heaven, to the *dueño del santo mundo,* and to the saints. Sojuel was the father of the *zajorines,* and that is why all he offered as *costumbre* (sacrifice) was well received by the God of heaven, by the saints, and by the *dueño del mundo.*

Again, it is said that he received the advice of the saints and of the god of the rain, who said:

Francisco, your *costumbres* are well received. Keep offering more. This will be for the good of you and your family. In the time of the punishment, when the people of the town lose their cultivations for lack of rain, it will be a punishment sent by the God of heaven and the God of the earth; the people will purge their rebelliousness, disobedience, drunkenness, adulteries, robberies, and slayings for two years. During the two years, I will take care of your cultivations, you will receive good crops, and you will help many of those who pay attention.

Francisco Sojuel in turn told the people to take care of the corn and beans, to have more respect, and to kiss the *santo mundo* [sacred earth] so that all would be forgiven. But the people continued with impenetrable (strong) hearts. Few paid any attention to Francisco Sojuel's advice.

The first year arrived. People were waiting for the rain in order to begin to sow, but it didn't rain. Many of the people planted the seed of the corn in dry earth. They also planted *güisquiles* [chayotes], *ayotes* [gourds, pumpkins], and *chilacayotes* [very large gourds fed to livestock], but the seed did not germinate for lack of rain.

Francisco Sojuel, they say, had a very big piece of land on the skirt of the volcano. He and his children went to plant corn, beans, *chilacayotes, camotes* [sweet potatoes], *ayotes,* and *güisquiles.* And they sowed it in dry earth. In eight days, they went to look at the plants. Already, they were very big. They had already begun to grow.

In the afternoons, sprinkles fell on the edges of the volcano where Francisco Sojuel had planted his crops. Only there fell the band of sprinkles. On the land of others, the seeds usually did not germinate, and where they did, they dried out from lack of moisture.

Thus it was the first year. Much hunger was felt in Santiago [Atitlán], and great sickness fell on the people. Many died of smallpox and measles.

Francisco continued offering *costumbres* to the great God of heaven and to the great *dueño* of the sacred earth. He also offered *costumbres* to the saints, to San Simón [Maximón], and to the god of the rain.

So it was during the two years. Francisco Sojuel and his family received crops in abundance, and none of them got sick. But it is said that he helped many of his people—that is, the good people, those who listened to his advice.

Then it is said that evil people joined together. The *zajorines, brujos, characoteles,* and other bad people of different *naguales* committed a big calumny against Chico [short for Francisco] Sojuel. These people at once went to complain to the office of General Ubico, saying, "Francisco Sojuel is a demon who has bewitched many people, and he called evil on the town." They also said that Francisco Sojuel pretended, or believed himself, to be a prophet. The general, it is said, became really angry and ordered the calvarymen to arrest Francisco Sojuel and take him to jail in Sololá. The mounted soldiers arrived to get Francisco, and they carried him to jail.

Francisco was separated from the other prisoners. His punishment was severe. They gave him a piece of bread and a glass of water for each meal. But Francisco Sojuel had a stronger power because of his *nagual.* In jail he didn't feel hunger or thirst. The guards of the government were waiting for the day that the prisoner would die. But Francisco Sojuel, well fortified with thirteen *naguales,* always went very calmly to his town to eat peacefully at his house with his family, without the guards realizing that he had left the jail. He left the jail of Sololá with the power of his *nagual,* a hummingbird, and thus he entered in the form of a hummingbird. But, it is said, when he departed from the jail, he was replaced by Santiago or by San Simón [Maximón]. Better said, when Francisco Sojuel left jail in the form of a hummingbird, Santiago or San Simón was the one who stayed in jail, taking the appearance of Sojuel, so that the other prisoners would not give the alarm that Sojuel had escaped.

Thus, Francisco Sojuel left jail in the form of a hummingbird, but since he entered his town in his natural form, his enemies saw him. Each time they got mad and repeated their accusations because this damned man walked free; or, better said, the people had no regard for this man.

General Ubico many times ordered other guards to see if what the enemies of the prisoner said was true, but each time the guards informed him that the prisoner, Francisco Sojuel, was seen in jail. President Ubico got very mad. He thought the enemies of Chico Sojuel were deceiving him and ordered that they be shot. But the story says that General Ubico didn't want to sign for the liberty of the prisoner Francisco Sojuel. Thus passed the days and the months.

One night, it is said, the *dueño* of the earthquake arrived at the jail to say to Francisco, "Sojuel, Sojuel, get up! Put on your *caites* [open-toed sandals] and tie your traditional pants with your *faja* [cloth belt, sash]. Get ready to leave! I'm going to cause an earthquake, destroy this jail, and kill the prisoners and guards."

"Very well," said Sojuel, and he did what the *dueño* of the earthquake said. A while after Sojuel left the jail, an earthquake knocked it down. The prisoners, guards, and everyone else died, except Sojuel. By dawn the next day, everything had crumbled. The political boss was astonished at the amount of damage because the earthquake he felt seemed to be of little intensity. The same political boss of Sololá sent messengers to the towns in order to advise relatives of the dead prisoners so that they would be able to search for the dead below the debris.

They say the relatives of Chico Sojuel arrived to look for his body, but when they arrived in Sololá, he was seated in front of the church. He told them everything that had happened, and then he told his family to wait a minute.

He went inside the church and changed into a *nagual,* and when he came out he was a beautiful woman. He did this to mislead the guards. The family knew that their father had taken the form of a woman, and they went together toward Santiago [Atitlán].

Later, when his enemies realized that Francisco Sojuel was still alive, they sent another complaint to the political boss of Sololá and to the president of Guatemala. Immediately, the general ordered the political boss of Sololá to send a platoon of horse soldiers to shoot Sojuel. Well, the soldiers headed to Santiago [Atitlán] to the house of the Tzutuhil, and again they grabbed him when he was sleeping and tied him to a post in front of the church.

In the morning all the people gathered in front of the town to witness the shooting, but no one could say anything. In that time it was dangerous to speak badly of the government. His enemies were very happy. But there were many more people in his favor because he had done nothing wrong in the town. They, however, could not ask the soldiers not to shoot him. They concentrated only on asking God to spare the life of their compatriot. The jefe of the soldiers said to the people that they were only fulfilling an order of the government.

The moment of the execution was the most painful for the *Atitecos*. It is said that Francisco Sojuel, with his face toward the church, was making the sign of the cross with his hands over his chest. Then the soldiers aimed their weapons to shoot, but not one of them discharged. They were replaced by others, and the same thing happened—their weapons did not fire. The jefe thought it was the fear of the soldiers, and then he stepped up to execute the criminal. But the same thing happened—his weapon did not function. The people present began to cry—some from sadness, others from happiness. It was not known what was happening.

When the soldiers saw that they could not shoot the *Atiteco,* they became really angry, seeing that indeed there were many people in favor of him. The jefe gave the order to tie him to the rear of a horse and drag him. They thus tied one end of a lasso to his neck and another to the rear of the horse for a horrible death.

The soldiers left town, dragging Señor Francisco Sojuel. It was well seen that the soldiers dragged him. They saw his form, but it was not he. It was his clothing but not his body. They say that when they dragged him to a place called Xecumuc, the solider untied the rope from the rear of the horse to examine the dead person, but when they looked, it was not Francisco Sojuel. The rope was tied only to a shaft and dry banana leaves, although indeed his clothes remained. The jefe and the soldiers cursed themselves because they didn't know what he had done or how he had escaped from the rope.

Very calmly, Francisco Sojuel arrived with his family to relate everything that had happened to him. His enemies would not be able to kill him because he possessed thirteen *naguales*. Neither hunger, nor firearms, nor being dragged by a horse could kill him. He said he was going to die but only when God wished him to do so and when the *dueño del santo mundo* said so. He, however, would not die once and for all. His spirit always would be with the people, and he would be reincarnated when they needed him.

Again, his enemies came back to accuse him before the military. The soldiers were again very angry, and they came to arrest him. They carried him to the *bartolina* [small and dark prison cell] in Sololá.

It is said the president ordered that they pour a lot of water in the *bartolina* until it reached the prisoner's belt so that [in that manner] he would die there. Neither his family nor his friends could visit him. Everything was forbidden. They could not bring food. He stayed enclosed in the *bartolina* with half his body in the water. When the guards came to examine him, he had hardly suffered. He always left the *bartolina* when he wished. He would go for a walk in Guatemala. In Mazatenango he would go to visit his relatives at night.

One time he met some compatriots in Quezaltenango. They were amazed and said, "Chico Sojuel, what are you doing here? We know that you are supposed to be in jail in Sololá. How can you be here, taking a walk?"

He answered, "Amigos, nothing bad has been done in our town. I am a person who has many amigos. Although some enemies are doing a lot of damage to me, the God of heaven and the *dueño del santo mundo* are with me. I only have come to greet you. Take much care; who knows when we will meet again?" He kissed the earth and disappeared instantly.

His friends were really astonished. Now they did not eat or sleep. They only kept thinking that they had talked with Francisco Sojuel. They knew that this hombre was imprisoned in the *bartolina* in Sololá. When those friends arrived in Santiago [Atitlán], they went to tell the townspeople that they had seen and chatted with Francisco Sojuel in Quezaltenango.

Chico's last feat, it is said, was to open a hole in the earth, make all the water that the guards had poured in the *bartolina* disappear, and very calmly leave jail. The guards tried many times to pursue him in order to kill him, but it was not allowed. When the pursuers arrived at his house, he transformed himself into some object—a cat, a dog, or a pretty woman. He transformed himself into many *naguales*. In the end, the soldiers and guards were unable to do anything. Francisco Sojuel died a natural death, but there is a majority of the people of Santiago Atitlán who believe that Francisco is their father and lord. They venerate and respect him like a saint. They say that Sojuel appears when he wants to and when the town needs him.

They say that especially when the soldiers were massacring many Indians in that town, Francisco Sojuel appeared to many inhabitants and told them that the military would have to abandon Santiago [Atitlán], the town would have to obtain peace, and the guerrillas would have to harvest their crops for the good of the poor people.[47] For these reasons, the people of Santiago now have Francisco Sojuel as a prophet.

The group Ixim Achá (*Hombres de maíz* [Men of Corn]) and the group Ajtzujila (*Flor de maíz* [Flower of Corn]) two years ago produced a cassette in the Tzutuhil language in which they relate and lament the anecdotes about the *principal* [town elder] Francisco Sojuel. Those two groups of folklorists say that when they begin to perform, their theme song is "Apalas Sojuel," which is to say, "For you, Francisco Sojuel."[48]

Teodoro Ujpán Batz[49]

Story of the Emigration and
Tragedy of a Cakchiquel People

The story goes like this. The founders of what is now called San Marcos la Laguna were of the Cakchiquel race, who more or less than four hundred years ago established their town, which was called San Marcos Paquip, at the foot of the volcano of San Lucas Tolimán. The mountain was pristine, and those who came to inhabit it were called the *Marqueños* [people of San Marcos].

The story says that they previously lived in a place that was called Pan Poj, but due to the big, strong currents of water that proceeded from the hills, their *ranchos* [rustic dwellings, cane huts] were knocked down and swept away by the rivers. Many of [the people] died. Those who lived were preoccupied with abandoning Pan Poj, and they moved to live in Paquip. They began to prepare the place; they cleared the trees and built their *ranchos* of leaves and branches.

But they say that in the nights they could not sleep because of the plague of mosquitos. At night, they had to burn much firewood to drive away the plague. Only then could they sleep a few hours. But many of them fell sick. Many of the children and women died. The men spent their days sick. Now they were not able to plant or work. It was agony. They felt too much hunger, and out of pure necessity they had to eat the roots of the trees.

With the passage of time, from the mountains, coast, and volcanoes of Santiago and San Lucas, came jaguars, mountain lions, and dangerous monkeys who ate up many *Marqueños*. By day and at night it was always dangerous for them. In the nights they had to stay together to sleep. When people wanted to leave to urinate or take care of their physical necessities, they had to be careful to look out for one another. If they did not, they would not return. When the women went to fetch water from the river, they had to be guarded by the men, who carried big, pointed stakes in order to drive off the monkeys who wanted to catch the women to have sex with them.

And so it went. Many of them were devoured by mountain lions and jaguars; they were almost annihilated. The few that stayed met and planned to abandon the place, so that they would not all die. They voiced their alarm, requesting aid from the governor of Santiago [Atitlán], who was called Jerónimo.

The governor had compassion for those of Paquip. He listened to everything that they had been suffering, and he gave them the authorization to occupy Tzan

Petey, which now is called Cerro de Oro [Hill of Gold], lands that belong to the Tzutuhiles of Santiago.

Well, the story says that the Tzutuhiles understood the pain that the Cakchiqueles were suffering. They were not in opposition, and besides, it was also the order of the governor. There, for a time, the *Marqueños* remained fairly content and in peace. They were hardly bothered by the *Atitecos* [people of Santiago Atitlán] who had planted *güisquiles* [chayotes], *ayotes* [gourds], *camotes* [sweet potatoes], yuca, and corn in Tzan Petey. The *Santiagueños* [people of Santiago] took good care of their crops because they lived off them.

But the story says those of San Marcos Paquip didn't like to work [in that area], and they did not have anything to eat. Out of pure necessity, they began to steal *güisquiles* and *ayotes,* and they dug up the *camotes* and yuca. That was what the Tzutuhiles did not like—by day and at night, their crops were always lost.

One day the *Atitecos* got together in order to brutally attack the Cakchiqueles. One of them, a man named Marujuch', spoke. He was the best *brujo* [witch] who had the power to turn into a jaguar. He called on all the *brujos* and *characoteles* [persons who can turn into *naguales*] who had the power to convert themselves into jaguars, mountain lions, monkeys, and serpents to go to Tzan Petey at night in order to look after the crops of their people, so that no more would be lost.

They divided the work between them. They took turns at night. Those who had the power went; that is, the *brujos* and *characoteles* converted themselves into big animals and went to Tzan Petey, where the poor persons of Paquip were.

Those of Paquip were persecuted by the mountain lions, jaguars, and monkeys. They no longer could leave their *ranchitos* [little cane huts] at night. To leave was to surrender to the mouths of the big animals. Because they were pursued by the animals, they prayed to God. They asked themselves, "Why were we persecuted by mountain lions, jaguars, and monkeys when we were in Paquip? Why have they followed us here?" They thought they were the same animals, but no, the real animals stayed in the woods. The animals that persecuted them in Tzan Petey were the *brujos* and *characoteles* who were protecting the crops [of the *Atitecos*].

Many of the *Atitecos* who converted themselves into snakes were the ones who guarded the crops by day. When the poor folks of Paquip wanted to steal the *güisquiles* and *ayotes,* huge snakes came out. The unfortunate people were not allowed to eat.

The snakes got into the *ranchitos,* into the bedclothes, and between the blankets. When the women shook their bedclothes and blankets, they found big rattlesnakes, even ones with two heads. That caused fear and illness. Many died. The men wanted to kill the snakes, but they were not allowed to do so. They disappeared mysteriously, because truthfully they were not snakes—they were men transformed into snakes who did not leave those of San Marcos Paquip in peace. Every day the suffering they endured became greater.

The story says that they again voiced their need for help. Again, they wanted to abandon the place where they were, but none of the towns gave them a hand. Finally, the mayor of Sololá took pity on them because they were Cakchiqueles like his people. He called them and told them that they could occupy the place that was called Pantiox, next to a group of *Sololatecos* [people of Sololá] who lived there.

Again the *Marqueños* emigrated, this time to Pantiox.

There, for a while, *Sololatecos* and *Marqueños* remained in the same place. With the passage of time, however, the *Marqueños* got a bad idea. They wanted to seize the few lands and crops of the *Sololatecos*. Also, the *Sololatecos* felt bothered by the *Marqueños*. They didn't like their abuse.

The story says that the *Sololatecos* gathered together all the people of the *cantones* [barrios] of the main town. United, they could throw out the *Marqueños* from Pantiox. Thus it was that thousands and thousands of *Sololatecos* arrived and burned the *ranchos* and the clothes of the *Marqueños*. The poor people of San Marcos, with tears in their eyes, had to abandon Pantiox.

Requesting help, they emigrated again to the place named Chuasani in San Pedro la Laguna. But it wasn't for much time, only one or two months. The *Pedranos* [people of San Pedro] didn't want other people to occupy lands that belonged to them. During that time, the *Marqueños* slept under the trees. When they were asleep, the *Pedranos* threw water on them and burned chili very near them. It was a hardship for the people.

At night, the story says, the *Marqueños* left Chuasani. They settled in a place called Xenimabaj y Tzanjuyú, where they founded the [present-day] town of San Marcos la Laguna. [And that is where they remained, without further strife.]

Raúl Teodoro, Cakchiquel, and Valerio Teodoro, Tzutuhil

A Sacred
Story In earlier times, the story says, there lived a señora who was very obedient and respectful to her parents. Each time she got up in the morning, she greeted them with "*Buenos días* [Good morning]," and she kissed their hands. She did the same thing in the afternoon and at night. The life of the woman was of much obedience, and she respected people from the smallest to the biggest.

The woman was poor and had the misfortune of getting married to a man who also was poor. The husband looked for herbs in the mountains and sold them to the people in town. But one day the husband of the lady had the bad luck to be devoured by the jaguars and coyotes in the forest, and he didn't return to their home. The woman was left with two small children.

Seeing that her husband didn't come back, very early the next day the lady took their two children and went to the forest to search for him. She thought that perhaps he had fallen in some ravine, and to help him, she went to the woods, walking and walking and crying, "Atun (Antonio), Atun, where are you? Tell me if you are in some ravine or if you are injured with the machete. Or maybe you are entangled in some *bejucal* [patch of lianas]." The unfortunate lady was speaking and shouting, but no one answered. She was with their two children, walking in the forest in search of her husband, but she could not find him. [As it was] already night, she returned to her house very tired.

The lady was crying and crying, but from so much fatigue she fell asleep. In a dream her husband appeared, saying, "My beloved wife, I know that you are very tired and sad from looking for me so much. You passed by very close to me. I am a little more to the right side."

In her dream, the woman answered her husband, "Atun, what have you done to us? Why don't you talk to us? Your children and I have been searching a lot for you. You are ungrateful. You have made us suffer all day."

The husband replied to his wife, "I will no longer come here, nor will I sell herbs anymore. The only thing I really recommend is that you take good care of our two children, and they will take care of you when they are grown."

Then the woman woke up, thinking it was real, but it was only a dream. The story says that it was the spirit of the husband that came to communicate to his wife, because the body had already been devoured by the animals in the forest.

At sunrise, the lady, together with her two small children, again took the road to the forest to search for her husband. In the woods she was shouting, "Atun, Atun, where are you? Here I am with your two children. We are looking for you." But there was no response.

Then the señora did what she had dreamed, going more to the right side where she had not passed the previous day, and exactly in that spot she found the bones of her husband, mutilated by the animals, the skull almost pulverized. She recognized him by his clothes. She found his machete, his *caites* [open-toed sandals], and the load of herbs that now was withered by the sun. The lady said, "This is my husband, and I kiss his bones." She gathered them together and left them below a big rock.

Crying, she told her two children:

My children, this happened to us because we are poor. Your *papá* came here to look for herbs in this forest. Now, he is already dead, eaten by the animals. Undoubtedly, the mountain lions and coyotes did it. Such is the life of us poor folks. Only God can help us.

So went the lady with her two children. They returned to their house crying, now without a husband and father. The lady stayed with her two small children; she could hardly work. She was very poor and barely able to feed them. She could not buy corn for tortillas, and she fed them only herbs every day.

With the passage of time, the two children grew up to be little youngsters who could do some work. They helped their *mamá* earn [money] for tortillas each day. But the story says that the youngsters were highly respectful and obedient, more so than the other young people of the town. The two youngsters were full of virtue and wisdom that the God of the heavens and the earth conceded to them. But in the towns there was much wickedness; the people didn't remember God. There was much adultery, drunkenness, robbery, and killing among the people.

The story says that God sent two castigations over the earth. The first castigation was to stop the rain, and now it didn't rain anymore over the earth. The clouds disappeared completely. The rivers ran dry. The crops dried out, and no longer was there corn or beans. It was a calamity of drought and hunger.

The second castigation was to make the night disappear. Now there was no darkness. Now the cool night air did not come. Everything was day.

More was the cry of the people because of the hunger and the thirst, but the people were not allowed to die, only to suffer for their sins. However, the animals—dogs, hens, and horses—were allowed to die [and escape the suffering] because they hadn't sinned.

The story says that the señora and her two children felt the same calamities of the hard life, but for them it was the same as before. They already were very poor—they already knew poverty and already lived a difficult life. Other people, who had been unaccustomed to hardship, ate horses, dogs, and hens that had died out of pure necessity from the hunger they endured.

One day the two youths heard a voice that said: "Don't eat what the people are eating. This is happening to them because of their wickedness. Tell your *mamá* to put the clay jar on the fire and look for small stones in the shape of little tamales. Begin to cook these stones, and you will see what will happen." And so they did.

When they told their mother what they had heard, the señora put the clay pot on the fire and put in it some stones the children had gathered in wooden crates. She then began to cook the stones. Suddenly they heard another voice that told them: "Brighten up! You are not going to suffer hunger or thirst. Put a gourd container in the corner of the *ranchito* [little cane hut], and you will have sufficient water." And so they did.

An hour after they put the stones in the pot and began to cook them, the tortillas emitted a pleasant aroma. But it was only small stones that they had put on the fire. The señora, crying out to God, took the pot out of the fire. When they opened the pot, the youngsters and their mother marveled that it was full of little tamales, which had been transformed from the stones.

Giving thanks to God, they began to eat the little tamales. It was the same when they went to inspect the gourd jar—it was full of water, and it did not end. They drank the water and took a bath, and still plenty of water remained. It was the same when the tamales were finished—the muchachos went to collect more small rocks to cook, and they had plenty of tamales.

For them life was better than before because before they ate only herbs. But when God sent the two punishments to earth, he had compassion for them because they were people who were respectful and fearful of him. For that reason, God gave them the power to turn the stones into food.

On the other hand, the other people were shouting and cursing themselves. They complained about hunger—men, women, and children, crying. They wanted to eat, but they did not have corn or beans. The clouds had disappeared, and all the crops had dried out for lack of rain. The worst misfortune was that there was no longer night, only day. The heat of the sun intensified; it was burning hot. The people wanted to rest below the trees, but the trees had lost their leaves from the force of the sun and extreme dryness.

The people criticized the señora and her two children because they felt neither hunger nor thirst. Their life was better than before.

One day, the story says, the señora and her youngsters left for the field to look for firewood. Without locking the house, they left the clay pot full of little tamales and the gourd full of water. Without concern, they went in search of firewood.

The people of the town entered the *ranchito* and discovered the secret. They found the jar of tamales and the gourd of water, and they began to eat and drink, finishing all of it and leaving only the empty gourd and jar. When the woman and her two children arrived, there no longer were little tamales or water. The people shouted that they wanted more.

The youngsters and the mother cooked more small stones that again were converted into little tamales. Also, they got more water from the gourds that again refilled with water. The people of the town wanted to do the same things but could not. They began to cook stones, but when they took them out of the fire, they were the same—stones. That is when they believed that the woman and her two children were true children of God.

The boys and the señora told the people that they should repent for their wayward ways. The people had to obey because [on their own] they were able to do nothing.

Suddenly [one day] the muchachos heard another voice that told them, "Go very far into the woods, and each one of you carry a gourd jar! There in the forest you will find the darkness and the clouds—these two you will find lying in a ravine."

Well, the two boys told the people what they had heard. The people said they would pay homage. They asked them to please go bring the clouds so that it would rain and they would have shade. Also, they asked them to please go fetch the darkness so that night would come back and they could be able to sleep.

"Fine, we're going to do the job," they said, and they said good-bye to their mom. Each carried a gourd jar. They went walking and walking many days in the forest, finally reaching a ravine where people had not been. There, lying in the ravine, they saw the clouds and the darkness. Very near them they put down their two open gourd jars.

Then the story says that the darkness, in the form of black air, went inside one of the gourd jars. The same thing happened with the clouds. They, in the form of white air, went inside the other jar. Then the two youths corked the two gourds and returned to their town.

When they arrived, they called for all the people to come and observe what each jar contained. They opened the first jar, and clouds began to come out of it. They covered the [dried] streams and hills—everything was covered with clouds. Then they opened the second gourd jar, and darkness began to come out of it. Night returned, [and it rained] until the people were content.

And the clouds and darkness did not end again. As for these two muchachos, one was then called *dueño* [owner, lord] of the clouds and the other was then called *dueño* of the darkness.

Ignacio Bizarro Ujpán

The Fisherman
and the King
In the past there lived a very poor but clever muchacho whose parents died when he was very small. He had to seek a way to make a living; he thought it better to dedicate himself to being a hunter and fisherman. His weapon was the arrow; any kind of animal that he found he brought down with the arrow. He was also a fisherman, but he used neither a harpoon nor a fishhook. He went [to fish] with only a small ring that his father had left him as

an inheritance. By means of the power of the ring, he completely disappeared below the water without using oxygen.

The ring gave him power, and below the water, the muchacho said to the ring, "You are the inheritance from my father, and you have to help me. Please don't abandon me."

The ring responded, "Don't worry. I'll be with you in every situation, in happiness and in pain. Now, what do you want?"

"Please, I want you to play a [piece of] music so that the fish and other animals of the sea will be happy."

"Fine," said the ring, and it began with cheerful, but very cheerful, music.

And then came the big and tiny fish, who felt very happy as they were dancing around the boy. By means of the power of the ring, the fish stayed immobile [some] moments.

The young man grabbed the best fish, put them inside his sack, and took them to sell to the people. Thus he spent his life. He hunted birds in the trees and other animals, and he also sold the meat to the people. Everything was due to the power of the ring because the muchacho didn't miss a single shot. And so he was improving his life; already he had his little house and a little land, because his father had not left him a house or land or other things, only the ring.

But what the muchacho was doing did not suit the people of the town. He hardly suffered to earn a living, and they accused him before King Turin, saying:

O Majesty, we know that you have power over us, over the animals of the earth, even the fish of the sea. O great King Turin, you don't realize that the forests are being depleted of animals. The wild pigs, the deer, the *tepescuintes* [brown rodents with black stripes on their backs], and the big and small birds are being exterminated. The sea is becoming void of fish because a damned hunter and fisherman is obliterating them. O great King Turin, we beseech you to realize that in a generation, the forests will be without animals and the trees without birds. The immense sea is being depleted of fish.

But all of this was a slander; the muchacho was not capable of annihilating all the animals of the forests and by no means capable of decimating all the fish of the immense sea.

King Turin was more than angry upon hearing the words of the people, who blamed him for lacking authority in his reign. He got up from his throne, saying, "People of Sansiriwux, as for everything that they say about that damned fisherman, I will carry out justice; I am capable of burning him alive."

Then they went to bring the fisherman, and they presented him before the king, who interrogated him, saying, "What is your name, damned person? You know that your life is in my hands. I can let you live, or I can burn you alive."

The boy answered, "I am called Ton Tun. I am a poor youth, but I'm not hurting anyone."

The king said:

How dare you exterminate all the animals of the forest and the fish of the sea. Don't you know that I am the great King Turin who can cremate you right now in a hot oven? But first I will impose a penalty. If you really are a hunter, bring me a dead jaguar here in my palace. I will spare your life but on the condition that this animal inflict no damage upon me or my soldiers, because if the animal does any harm, I will order that you be burned.

But the king knew that in the forest there was not a single jaguar, only smaller species [of animals].

"O King, I will carry out the order. I will return within five days." The unfortunate muchacho left sad, thinking about how to save his life. He knew that in that place there were no mountain lions or jaguars. His only comfort was the ring.

He walked and walked in the forest for three days and nights, but not a single jaguar could he find. Tired, on the third night he said to the ring, "Inheritance from my father, help me. If you don't help me, the king is going to burn me alive."

The ring spoke, saying, "Amigo, your father has told me to never let you die. I will help you, and you will always be the winner. The orders of the king are like foam [of the sea; that is, insignificant]. Right now I am going to play the drum and the chirimía [wind instrument similar to an oboe] so that all the animals of the enchanted places come to dance here in this place, but be ready with your arrow."

In a little while, so pleasant was the sound of the drum and the chirimía that the animals gathered, large and small, including the mountain lion and jaguar, and they began to dance happily. As soon as the animals were content, the young man took out his arrow and inserted it in the eye of the jaguar, and the animal fell dead.

The boy felt incapable of carrying the jaguar because it was heavy. It was the ring that gave him enough strength to carry the jaguar on his back to the palace of the king. There he said, "O great King Turin, here is the jaguar you asked me for." The frightened king thought that he was seeing some vision, because there was not another man like the muchacho. He had gone to hunt a jaguar, and he had brought it on his back from the forest to the palace.

The king got up from his throne, shaking his finger and realizing what he saw was true, and said to the muchacho, "Young man, you are a demon. Naturally you are finishing off the small animals, and what you now have for me is a jaguar. Bring this animal back to life!"

The boy, trembling and thinking that the ring had abandoned him, approached where he had stretched out the jaguar and blew on the eye where he had inserted the arrow. The jaguar moved, gradually supported himself over his four paws, and came back to life, licking his snout, moving his tail, and making gestures as if he would like to eat the king. The frightened king took off running from his throne and said to the muchacho, "Save me from this animal so that he doesn't harm me. I am an innocent king. Others are the ones who accuse you. Please take this wild animal out of my palace before I die of fear."

The muchacho without fear caressed the jaguar, making signs that he follow — the hunter in front, the jaguar behind like a dog — and they went to the forest. The hunter said to the jaguar, "Thank you, amigo jaguar. You saved me from death. The king wanted to burn me alive."

The jaguar did the same, making signs with his head and tail, as if he wanted to say, "Thank you for having carried me to the palace of a king, and thank you for a new life." But the enemies of the hunter didn't remain satisfied with the punishment that the king gave him, murmuring that he had defrauded them by not applying true justice. And they arrived again at the palace, saying, "O Great King, the people of Sansiriwux know very well when a king offers justice. This deserves respect, but you now have defrauded your people."

The king, seeing that nobody was in his favor, promised them another justice, and he sent for the soldiers again to capture the young hunter. Again the boy was brought to the palace of the king. King Turin proclaimed, "Damned fisherman, for your guilt the people have revolted against my reign. I now will sentence you."

The young hunter very calmly and respectfully answered, "O Majesty, I am doing nothing wrong, as they are accusing me. I am only a poor hunter and fisherman."

Again the king had compassion, seeing the humility and the respect of the young hunter. In order not to burn him alive, he passed another sentence.

The king said to the soldiers, "Carry two axes without handles and my ring of gold that have my name engraved on them and let them fall to the depths of the sea, but with care that the damned hunter not know where."

"Very well, we will carry out the order," replied the soldiers, and they did what the king commanded.

The king again said to the young fisherman:

Young man, since you like to go below the water a lot, I will now be able to hand down your sentence. In the depths of the sea you will find two axes without handles that have my name engraved on them and my ring of gold that has my portrait and my name engraved on it. You must find them and bring them to me. If you don't bring them to me within three days, you will be burned in an oven heated seven times with firewood and sulfur.

Crying, the young fisherman left the palace. He didn't know what to do, and he headed for the seashore. To make things worse, the ring had disappeared for one day. Seated in the sand crying, he could not go below the water without the ring.

While he was crying, the ring appeared. And it told him, "Muchacho, why are you sad and crying? Don't cry anymore. Never will I leave you. I will be looking after you until the last days of your life. I departed for a moment, but I am here now. Let's go below the sea to search for the king's two axes and the ring."

"But how can I search for those things? I don't have much strength to submerge to the greatest depths of the sea," said the muchacho.

"Let's go. Don't be afraid," said the ring, and they went below the sea. They traveled really far, but they didn't know where to look for the axes and the ring.

When they were far out [into the sea], the ring created really delightful music. Then the big and tiny fish began to arrive, as if they were dancing around the fisherman. And suddenly an hombre appeared dancing with the fish, but he was different.

The fisherman spoke to him, saying, "Hombre, who are you? I didn't know there were men like you below the sea."

The other person answered, "I am the *dueño* [master, god] of the sea; mine are all the fish and other animals that live here in the sea. And you, who are you?" asked the *dueño* of the sea.

The muchacho answered, "I am an unfortunate fisherman who is suffering the punishment of a king. I am searching for two axes and a ring of gold that have the name of the said king engraved on them. He says that they can be found in the depths of the sea, but I can't find anything."

The *dueño* of the sea said, "Don't worry. Quit crying, don't be sad. I will call to all the live creatures that live in the sea and order them to search for the two axes and the ring."

The *dueño* of the sea called the sharks, the whales, and all the species of animals that live in the sea and ordered them to look for the two axes and the ring. All the animals of the sea, big and small, very obediently went to all the depths of the sea.

Three tiny fish found what they were searching for, but they could not hold onto them because they were too small. They had to advise the big fish. In a joint effort by many of them, the two axes and the ring were carried and delivered to the *dueño* of the sea.

"Amigo, here are the two axes and the ring of the king. Your life is saved by us creatures who live in the sea. Go and hand them over to the king, but don't tell what you experienced here." The young fisherman, very content, thanked the *dueño* of the sea and left.

Again he presented himself to King Turin to deliver the two axes and the gold ring. The great King Turin was astonished because there was no man who could search for things in the depths of the sea. Again, he spared the life of the young fisherman. The muchacho again left the palace very content, giving thanks to God for having received a pardon from the king.

But his enemies remained unsatisfied with the measures of the king. They presented themselves again at the palace and introduced a new accusation, saying to the king, "Your majesty, O King Turin, the damned fisherman laughs at your majesty and your orders. He says that he is a man stronger than a king and that when he wants to, he will take over your reign. You will be overthrown."

Upon hearing this, the king got up from his throne, grinding his teeth like an angry bull, and ordered that the poor fisherman be brought for another sentencing. And the king said, "Damned fisherman, because of you I can't find peace with my people. You are a disgrace to your parents. Confess if it is true that you now laugh and make fun of my reign. Right now I am ordering your head to be cut off."

The unfortunate man answered in a low voice and with tears in his eyes, "O Great King, never have I deceived you or laughed at Your Excellency. I am innocent of what they accuse me of!"

Hearing the words of the fisherman, the king acted pompously as he judged whether the muchacho was innocent or guilty. To calm the animosity of the people, he imposed another punishment, declaring under oath that it was the last fine and the last pardon he could earn. If he won, his enemies would be beheaded, but if he lost, his head would be cut off.

Then came the last punishment. The king called four soldiers and told them, "Walk ten days in the forest. Carry my crown and my wife's ring. Leave my crown hidden in a place where people have not been and leave the ring at the top of a tree so that nobody can see them." The soldiers did everything that the king ordered, and they told him his command had been fulfilled.

Then the king said to the fisherman, "You have only five days, and when you return I want you to bring me my wife's ring and my crown. Go and look for them in the forest. In this manner you will have either life or death."

Very forlorn, the unfortunate man left the palace. He didn't know which road to take. He was sad and crying because his life was full of only false accusations. He took the road to the forest, but when he arrived in the woods, in the direction where he was going, he became completely disoriented. Again he spoke to the ring: "Ring, inheritance from my father, without your aid, the king will cut off my head."

Then the ring spoke to the muchacho: "Go farther into the woods! Don't be afraid! The animals will help you. When you are in an immense forest where the rays of the sun can no longer be seen, by means of the power of the ring, there will be the sound of the drum and the *chirimía,* more beautiful than the animals have ever heard."

Then the big and tiny animals began to arrive, among them the jaguar and the mountain lion, the bear, and the elephant.[50] They happily danced, and suddenly among the animals appeared a man dancing like the animals. He spoke to the hunter: "Young man, why are you sad? Can't you see that the animals and I are very happy?"

The hunter answered, "I have problems in my life. The king handed down a final sentence. He said that here in the forest I have to search for his crown and his señora's ring, but I don't know where to find them. I have only five days of life left if I don't find what I'm looking for."

The hombre answered, "Young man, I am the king of the animals. With much pleasure I will help you. Right now I will send all the animals to go to look for the crown and ring."

The king of the animals ordered all of them, large and small, to search for the crown and ring. After searching for one day and one night, the *tepescuinte* found the crown, and the monkey found the ring on a very big tree. The animals very happily carried back the crown and ring and delivered them to the king of the animals. Then the king of the animals gave them to the young fisherman. Much obliged, the young fisherman jumped with joy and ran to the palace of the king to present the crown and the ring that would save his life.

The king observed that everything the people had said against the muchacho was false, and he gave the order for all of them to be decapitated because of their lying tongues.

Colorín colorado, this story has finished; to he who tells me a story, I will tell two.

Ignacio Bizarro Ujpán

Story of
the Owl As a very old story goes, our old folks of earlier times and those of present times maintain the idea that one must be careful not to kill owls, because they are guardians and policemen of the world. They only follow orders of the *dueño del mundo* [owner, god of the world, earth]. That is why when one comes into a homesite or alights and hoots above the house of a person, the person must not bother it, because if one bothers or hurts an owl, that person can easily die within a few days.

The story goes that at one time an owl landed upon the *rancho* [cane hut, rustic house] of a family. Every night, there it was perched and hooting, but the animal was disquieting. The family no longer could sleep peacefully, for the animal had no fear of them. First they scared him off by throwing stones and sticks at him, but the creature always came back to hoot on the *rancho*. Without any other remedy, the man grabbed a shotgun and shot him directly.

But the story goes that he could not kill him at once. The owl was still alive but seriously wounded, with a broken claw and wing. It managed to arrive at the location of the *dueño* of the enchanted place, from which the owls are sent on errands to investigate all the wickedness people do in the nights and also to see how many are ready to die. The *dueño del mundo*, it is said, controls everything.

Five days after the man had wounded the owl, he grabbed his lasso, porter's strap, machete, and ax, and he went to the hill to look for firewood. When he was beginning to cut his firewood, the story says that at his side suddenly appeared a tiny young man, very blond and of very small stature, who spoke to the lumberjack. "Señor, those sticks are very hard. Your arms will get tired. But there, up above, I have firewood. I'll give you a *tercio* [portion of firewood a man can carry on his back]. Come. Follow me."

The timberman thanked and followed the young man. They climbed until reaching the peak of the hill. But the little man's words were lies—there was no firewood, just deceit. It was like the art of magic when the woodcutter realized he was already seeing strange things.

The young man said, "Here it is different. You have to see many more things."

It was clear, the story says, but one could not see the sun. There were thousands and thousands of animals: deer, jaguars, mountain lions, coyotes, monkeys, raccoons, wildcats, and many more animals. But they were corralled. They didn't have liberty because if they were freed, the people would finish killing them off, and more for that reason, they were well protected.

With the señor leading the way, the lumberman was taken to the *dueño* of the Pulchich Hill, a very fat man with a very angry appearance. He had only four teeth, two up and two on the side below.

The woodcutter felt very scared. The enchanted person spoke: "Hombre, what are you doing here? Who brought you?"

The lumberjack answered, "A young man brought me here by deception. He offered to give me firewood, but I now feel disoriented. I don't know where I am."

The *dueño* said, "There is no problem here. You must stay here for four hours. You owe me the life of one of my policemen, guardians of the world. You remember when you wounded an owl with your shotgun? The animal had done no harm to you. He was completing a mission."

The *dueño* of the hill sent for the owl that was wounded. The story says the poor thing was very injured in the wing, with a broken leg that was draining pus (infected). The *dueño* of the hill very angrily grabbed a little of the material that was oozing out of the owl, put it in the mouth of the hombre, and asked him, "Do you approve of this, what you have done to this unfortunate animal? Within eight days you must come here to cure the injuries of this policeman and guardian of the world. Come!" he commanded, and he took him to show him the rest of the wounded animals and the men who were doctoring them. He also showed him other strange men who had been given severe punishments because they could not cure the animals that they had wounded when they were hunting in their previous lives. And the *dueño* said to the lumberman, "Here you will have to treat the owl, and if you are able to heal [him], your punishment will be less. But if you aren't able to heal him, your punishment will be three times greater, nothing more and nothing less. The owl owes you nothing, and it is a policeman and guardian of the world."

In a blink of an eye the lumberjack sensed that he was now in the place where he wanted to make firewood. The *dueño* of the hill told him that he had to be there for four hours. However, it was not four hours—it was four days.

The relatives and neighbors of the man went to search for him because it had been four days since he had disappeared. They thought that perhaps the river had carried him away, that he had fallen into some barranca, or that he might have been eaten by the animals.

In four days they found the lumberman coming down from Pulchich Hill. Together they brought him to his house, where he began to give them an account of what he had seen and what he had been told. The people of the town thought that the man was a little loco or that he wanted to upset them with all he was saying.

But the man was relating what he had experienced during the four days. And everything turned out to be true. In eight days the man died. Not until then did the people believe that what he had said was real.

Ignacio Bizarro Ujpán

The Sombrerón and the Blue Fly

Long, long ago a couple, neither rich nor poor, lived in a town.[51] They were Indians of Sololá. The woman, the story says, was called Micaela and the husband was called Pacheco. Their life was exemplary, but it was a pity that one day death separated them.

The husband loved and respected his señora very much, and the lady also respected and obeyed her husband. Their life was peaceful, like a gift from God.

At times problems arose in the family, but they resolved them with great patience. They raised their children with great kindness. But in time, to earn a living, the children went to live far away. Don Pacheco and Doña Micaela remained in their town. They were not old but of a good age when Doña Micaela took sick. The husband was very concerned for the health of his wife, and he spent his last centavos [to help her]. The man wanted his woman to improve. But the misfortune of the lady was to get worse each day, and she died. The husband didn't want his mate to die, but there was no remedy. He had to let go of her when she died in his arms. The hombre was strong and didn't want to tell his neighbors, still thinking that his spouse would revive. But all was useless, and she did not come back to life. Not until three days had passed did he advise the relatives and neighbors.

Well, the relatives and neighbors gave a good burial to Doña Micaela, and afterward they all went home. The unfortunate husband stayed in his house, alone, sad, and crying. There was nobody for him because the children had left to live far away. In his solitude, he cried day and night for his wife, many times saying, "Micaela, why did you go? Why did you leave me? Where are you? Speak to me! I can't live without you, nor can I forget our life together. Damned luck, why were you taken from my side? Right now I want to see and hug you." Not for a moment could the man forget his partner; out of sadness, he neither ate nor drank. He went to the places where he had been with his dead wife to see if he could see her in body or in spirit.

One day the solitary husband found himself in the forest, crying a lot and speaking to himself: "Micaela, I'll never forget you. In this place we looked for herbs. Here, we came to search for firewood." And he began to cry again.

While he was crying, a man suddenly arrived, mounted on a black burro. The man was dressed in trousers, shirt, and a big sombrero, all black in color. The man spoke to him, saying, "Hombre, quit crying. Now don't cry for your wife. She will never return. I am the *dueño* [master] and lord of death. With me are all the dead, and I have power over them."

And then Don Pacheco answered, "If you really are the *dueño* and lord of death, show me where my wife, Micaela, is, if only to see her. I can't live without her."

The *dueño* of death replied, "Very well, I will show you your woman, but you have to go on the butt of my donkey so that nothing will happen to you on the road. So that you can go on the butt of my burro, you have to transform yourself into a fly. Now do four turns on the floor with your head down and feet up."

"Very well, thank you. I will do it," the man said. Then he did the four turns on the floor, and he was transformed into a fly, but with reasoning like a man.

Then the story goes that the *dueño* of death was mounted on the burro and said to the fly-man, "Grab the rear end of my burro with your face [pointed] back so that you can see where we are going. Don't be afraid, and hold on tight."

"Very well," said the fly-man, and he grabbed onto the behind of the burro.

The donkey began to run very swiftly, as if it were flying. The fly-man saw that they passed through strange places, climbing up and going down mountains and rivers. The ass moved his hoofs, but they no longer were on the ground. Now they were flying in the air.

As they came to a strange place, the *dueño* of death descended and said to the fly, "Get off the butt of the burro and then [do] another four turns."

He did the four turns and stopped in his normal form. The *dueño* of death said, "Sad man, now we have arrived. Here is the place of the dead. They all come here. You can walk around in this place. You have three days and three nights to be here and find your woman. Go look for her."

The sad man found himself in a place where neither the bark of a dog nor the song of a bird was heard. It was completely silent, but a great, fearful silence.

The man walked a little more ahead and saw a lot of people separated by distinct groups. Drunks who had died of drunkenness were separated from others who had died in accidents. He could see clearly the fractures and wounds inflicted on their bodies. But the truth is that they were not real corpses, only transparencies. They were ghosts.

Separated were the women who in this life had consented to prostitution. They received great punishments. Also separated were the *brujos* [sorcerers], the envious, and the liars, who were whipped by other men.

Those who had behaved well in this life were also separated. They were treated well. Many of them were clearing and sowing, others cleaning and picking flowers. Other groups were singing happily. There was a lot of joy among the last groups. In these groups, the señor found his woman but accompanied by a man. The husband was bothered and asked himself, "Who is this man? I don't know him."

He wanted to speak to his wife, but the woman no longer recognized him. Instead, she saw him as a stranger. But then three days and nights passed, and the man had to return to where the *dueño* of death was.

The *dueño* of death asked him, "Have you already visited your wife? Have you spoken to her?"

The man answered, "Señor, I saw my wife, but she didn't speak to me. She already has another husband. She has forgotten me. When she looked at me, I so much wanted to speak to her, but she acted as if she didn't recognize me."

The *dueño* of death said:

Don't be a fool. It is not another man or husband that she has. It's you. What you see is your ghost because within a few days you will be here with her. Your spirit is here with the spirits of the dead. Thus, since you soon will be with your wife, your sadness will be over. Right now I am going to return you to the place where I got you three days ago. Tell your relatives what you have seen and tell your friends to take care that they don't come here to suffer. Here, there is everything, suffering as well as eternal happiness. Take another four turns on the floor so that you again will change into a fly, and grab onto the behind of my donkey.

"Very well," he said.

He did the four turns, turned into a fly, and grabbed onto the bottom of the donkey. The *dueño* of death went mounted [on the donkey] for the return, passing through the same places.

When they arrived again, the *dueño* got down from the ass and told the fly, "Come down off the butt of my burro and do four turns so that you change into a man."

"Very well," said the fly.

He came down from the derriere of the donkey, did the four turns, and returned to his normal life. But at that instant he saw nothing. Who knows what the *dueño* of death did to disappear?

The man little by little descended from the hill to his town. Very frightened, he went into his *ranchito* [rustic house]. He didn't forget what he had seen and heard. He began to tell his neighbors, relatives, and friends, but they didn't believe it, thinking that perhaps he was joking.

In three days he fell sick with vomiting and diarrhea and died. Not until then did his neighbors, friends, and relatives believe that what the man had said was true. They wanted to ask him more, but it was impossible.

That is why we Tzutuhiles and Cakchiqueles call the fly of the flesh, or blue fly, the "eye of death."

Ignacio Bizarro Ujpán

Temperament and the Deeds of the Son of God

Long, long ago lived a poor, humble man who was the son of God, all powerful.[52] In his town he wanted to do something good, but the people scorned him and treated him like a lunatic.

The man, seeing that nobody in his town liked him, went wandering over all the earth, going through rivers, mountains, the rain, and many other things. Walking, he came across some men who were sowing wheat.

The son of God asked them, "Amigos, what are you planting?"

They responded [with deference], "Señor, we are sowing wheat."

"Very well," the man said. "From right now you will begin to harvest wheat."

He said good-bye to them and continued on his journey. In a short while, the men already were harvesting a beautiful wheat field, an enormous crop that no one could take care of because the granaries were already full with wheat here and there. The owners were happy, but they saw no more of that man who told them, "From right now you will begin to harvest wheat."

The man continued on his way and ran into others who were planting milpa.

"What are you planting?" he asked them.

With much appreciation and respect, they answered, "Señor, we are sowing milpa (cornfields), but only God can help us. Rain is very scarce."

The hombre, son of God, told them, "Harvest corn on this day and continue sowing with much abundance." Then he said good-bye.

When the planters looked behind, ahead, and to the sides, they already saw a beautiful cornfield. They were shouting, asking for help to put up the harvest. The people of the town were astonished. They asked the planters what they had done so that in only a single day they were planting and harvesting. It was very well known that all sown fields take three to six months to produce a crop. But the planters kept the secret. They didn't tell the people that the son of God had spoken to them.

The man with power passed through another town, walking and walking. There he met some pretentious and spiteful men.

"What are you working at?" he asked them, "I wish you luck."

Then one of those who was working responded, "Hombre, don't waste our time. We are planting. Go look for work!"

The man, son of God, replied, "Hombre, what are you planting?"

The other answered, "We are sowing stones."

"Then continue sowing stones, and stones you will harvest."

He continued on his way, and then the planters realized that everything they were seeing behind and ahead of them was stones—big and tiny stones. They no longer could pass, and the planters shouted and complained that they had lost their land, that they could not dig to plant a single sprig. Everything had been converted into rocks. That is why there now are many rocks—because of the envy and the wickedness of man.

In that same town but farther ahead, the son of God met other men who also were sowing.

"Amigos, what are you planting? A blessing for you, and may it multiply."

The men answered with scorn, "Beggar, why are you asking? We know what we are planting."

He answered them patiently, "What is it that you are planting?"

They responded, "We are sowing thorns and thistles."

He replied, "With abundance you will harvest thorns and thistles."

He continued walking. When the workers looked to their sides, everything was thorns and weeds (brambles). They could not pass. At the same time, the workers shouted that they had lost their lands. [This was] for answering him badly.

For that reason, when man plants his corn and beans, thorns and weeds grow with them as a punishment for man's arrogance.

The son of God continued walking and walking until arriving at another town. He noticed some men who were passing by in a large cornfield.

"Amigos," he inquired, "how good are the ears of corn? Give me one! I like roasted ears of corn." He told them this only in order to see if they were compassionate or ungrateful.

"We don't eat this," the men responded. "We planted it for the pigs, bulls, and horses."

The man, son of God, told them, "Well, let the animals eat it, and may they not get full. Let them eat by day and at night."

So he spoke and continued walking. In the blink of an eye appeared many pigs, bulls, and horses, eating the milpa. They finished it in less than two hours.

The owners of the milpa fought to get the animals out, but they could do nothing. What they had said was that they were planting the milpa for the animals. All was finished.

That is why they say that from the mouth comes blessings and curses, and that is why the pigs, horses, and bulls now eat by day and at night. And those animals never get full, however much they eat. They like to scour the crops of man as a punishment.

Since the man, son of God, did not have land or a house where he could rest, he spent his life walking and walking. The blessed man arrived in another town.

He was very tired from much walking. In that town he entered into the house of a man who was kneading bread.

"Blessed amigo," he said, "let this be your work from now on."

"Welcome, amigo," the baker answered. "Help me make bread. I need you to help. I have a lot of work." And he put a little piece of dough [in his oven].

The man, son of God, with the very small piece of dough, began to make bread. In a little while it began to grow as the baker had never before seen. Then they baked bread here and there. The house was filled with bread, but beautiful kinds of bread, better than any other baker could make them.

Then the man, son of God, said, "May this work be blessed and fruitful, may it be the food of all humanity, and may you not have an enemy in the world."

Then he continued on his journey.

This is the reason that bread is desired throughout the whole world. Blacks and whites, people of different religions, atheists, youngsters and adults, and the rich and poor—all eat it.

Colorín colorado, this story is by a Tzutuhil Maya called Ignacio Bizarro Ujpán.

Doña María and Her Three Children

In the past lived a married couple. The husband was called Señor Pancho, and the lady was called Señora María. Señor Pancho was a carpenter; Señora María was a midwife. In the town where they lived there was not much work. Don Pancho wanted to work in his carpentry profession, but clients didn't come because in the town where they lived all the people were poor.

Señora María wanted to use her knowledge as a midwife, but there wasn't much for her to do because in the town there were not many people. With the passage of time the señora gave birth to three children, but from bad luck Señor Pancho fell sick and died. Doña María was left with only her three small children. The señora cried by day and at night because she could not find work to earn sustenance for her three small boys. There were days when she obtained some tortillas and days when they ate only herbs. For her and her three children, life was an ordeal. By the great mercy of God, the children grew healthy and very robust. The first was called Gabriel, the second named Miguel, and the last christened Lorenzo. As they grew up, they were full of virtue.

The three were dreamers. Gabriel dreamed that he was elevated by the clouds to a very high place. Happily he passed over the towns, over the volcanoes, and over the seas. Thus was Gabriel's dream. Miguel dreamed that he was the *dueño* [owner, lord, master] of the cold and dumped a strong cold over the earth by his own power. And Lorenzo dreamed that he was *dueño* of the wind. He was carried by the wind, passing over lakes, seas, mountains, and cities. When he said, "*Hasta aquí* [until here]," the wind obeyed and calmed its forces. Every time that they dreamed, each one dreamed the same thing.

The three siblings asked their *mamá* if they had a virtue when they were born, because the three felt bothered by what they had dreamed in the nights. The mother gave an answer to her three children, saying:

Gabriel, I know that you have been born with good fortune. The hour when you were born, inside the *ranchito* [little rustic house] where we lived, you were covered with clouds, like a white cloud and fog. All those who witnessed your birth were scared because of everything they saw. But little by little the cloud and fog disappeared. That's what happened when you were born, Gabriel.

Now, you, Miguel, they say that when you were born was a very good day. I remember you were born in the afternoon. At the hour when you saw the light of the world for the first time, in the little house where we were, a great cold sprung forth. But what a cold! The relatives who were with me were all trembling from cold, an unbearable cold, but you didn't feel the cold. Little by little it returned to normal. This is what happened when you were born, Miguel.

Very well, Lorenzo, my last son, my little love, you too have been born with good fortune. Perhaps there is not another person in the world who has been born at that hour. You were born when the stars of the east illuminated the horizon, signaling the dawn of a new day, when the little birds with their song cooed to Heart of Heaven and to Heart of Earth. Well, it was in this hour when you were born, Lorenzo. In the *ranchito* where I gave birth to you, a very strong wind suddenly arose that whipped up inside and outside [the house]. Your grandmothers and your grandfathers were very frightened and almost suffocated from the strong wind. Thus it was. Little by little the wind calmed down.

The mother continued talking to her three sons:

Children of my dreams, children of my pain, children of my poverty and of my memories of youth, I now have told each one of you about the day when you were born. You have been born with very good fortune. But there is one thing. You yourselves have to search for the *suerte* [luck, fortune] that concerns each one of you, because if you do not look for it, you will not find it. God doesn't allow *suerte* to fall from heaven. You yourselves must search for it, and you must obtain it through struggling and suffering. I already told you that you have been born with very good virtue.

"Thank you, *mamá,*" said the three sons of the señora.

With the passage of time, the mother of the three young men died. They remained alone. None of the three wanted to look for a woman, because each had been born in order to live single, with a spiritual power.

Gabriel, Miguel, and Lorenzo, the three siblings, thought and said, "Our mother is now dead. Each one of us has to search for his *suerte.* We remember what she told us. We ourselves will have to seek our fortunes. We aren't going to wait for something from heaven, because God doesn't help the lazy."

Well, Gabriel took to the road and went walking in search of work, *suerte,* or fortune; that is, venturing. So it also was with Miguel and Lorenzo. They abandoned the house where they were born, and each one set off on the road. They walked for many days. Where night found them was where they slept. Sometimes they ate; sometimes they didn't. But during the nights when they slept, they always dreamed the same things as they had when they were at home.

Gabriel felt afraid. Every night he dreamed he was the *dueño* of the clouds, and he was carried by the same clouds to several places in the world. But when he woke up, it was only a dream.

Thus it also was with Miguel. Every night he dreamed that he was the *dueño* of the cold. In the dream he felt that he scattered a strong cold on the earth. But when he woke up, it too was only a dream. But he didn't find a way to interpret his dream.

Lorenzo dreamed that he was the *dueño* of the wind. He passed over the mountains, the lakes, the seas, and the highest hills. After a while he woke up, but it was only a dream. He felt that in his character there was something good, but he could not interpret the dream.

The three siblings traveled to different places, but they didn't go together. Each one went alone in search of his good fortune.

Gabriel, the oldest brother, struggled many days. He passed through many towns, but no one gave him work. He continued walking until he arrived on a very high hill. There night fell. Strengthened by his spirit, there he remained sleeping under a tree. At midnight came an old man, with a very fine face, as if it had been sprayed with cold air. His very fine hair and thick beard looked like silk, like velvet, as if they had been combed. The señor was the *dueño* of enchantment, and he spoke to Gabriel, saying, "Young man, why are you sleeping on this hill? This is my place, and it is very sacred."

Gabriel answered:

My señor, señor of white hair and a thick, white beard, I am sleeping here in this sacred place because night fell and I stayed here. My señor, I was walking, searching for my good *suerte.* Every night I dream I am walking on the clouds here and there. The clouds carry me to several parts of the world. My mother told me that I was born with good fortune but that I would have to leave to search for my *suerte*. We are three. My two siblings dream differently than I. Each one of us dreams the same thing over and over.

The señor of white hair and a thick, white beard replied to Gabriel, "I am the master and lord of all the beings that live on earth. I have power over everything. I am the *dueño* of the makers of rain, and I change the seasons. I take care of the clouds, and I take care of the cold and the wind. Now tell me about the dreams of your siblings!"

Gabriel retorted:

My brother Miguel, night after night, dreams that he is in charge of dumping cold over the earth. In the dream he looks at the people trembling with cold and at the animals [almost] dying of the sheer cold.

Now, the continual dream of my brother Lorenzo is that he goes up in the wind and he passes over the mountains, seas, and lakes. When he says, *"Hasta aquí,"* the wind obeys him.

"Very well," said the señor of white hair and a thick, white beard. "The fortune and the *suerte* of you three are in my hands. Return and bring your two siblings so that I can give them the power."

Gabriel answered, "My señor, my two siblings are lost traveling. We left the house together, but on the road each one went his own way, looking for his *suerte*. Now, who knows where they are?"

The señor said:

Some thieves killed your brother Miguel. In a three-day walk, you will find his body under a ceiba tree. There, make three crosses in the earth and say three times the name of your *mamá* and the name of your brother. He will get up then. I will be there, but you will not see me. When your brother is resuscitated, he will accompany you. Your brother Lorenzo you will find on the peak of the first volcano you encounter, but he also was devoured by a jaguar. His bones you will find below a canoj tree. Then join the bones of your brother. Place them with his face pointing to the east. On your knee, with your eyes closed, say the name of your mother thirteen times, the name of your brother thirteen times, and the name of your father thirteen times. I will be there, and I will resuscitate him. He's not dead; he's resting.

"Very well," said Gabriel. He left on his return. He walked three days and found the body of his brother Miguel below a ceiba tree. Then he did what he had been told on the hill. Miguel got his breath back and stood up. They greeted each other and began to walk again.

They had been walking for two days when they saw a volcano and began to climb it. When they arrived on the crest of the volcano, they found the bones of their brother Lorenzo under a canoj tree. Then Gabriel joined together the bones of their brother and placed them with the face to the east. Then he dropped to his knee and said the name of their mother thirteen times, the name of Lorenzo thirteen times, and the name of their father thirteen times. The two had their eyes closed. When they opened their eyes, Lorenzo was reincarnated—that is, returned to life. They greeted each other, and they were like they were before.

They took to the road again and spent a few more days going back to the hill of enchantment. There they slept below the trees. At midnight, out came the señor of white hair and a thick, white beard, *dueño* of the hill. He saw the three brothers and addressed their queries about their dreams, telling them, "Your *suerte* is in my hands. Here, you are going to work. Each one of you has his season for working. Gabriel, you have the power to make rain over the earth.[53] You'll have to walk on the clouds and do as I command."

"Very well, my señor," said Gabriel.

"Miguel, you have the power to make it cold on earth. I will tell you when to change the seasons.

"Lorenzo, in accordance with your dream, you have the power to make the wind blow from north to south and east to west. I will tell you when to change the seasons."

"Very well, señor of white hair and a thick, white beard, master and lord of this sacred place. We have to obey you. We will be at your service. We have been born in order to work according to our destiny," the three siblings said.

The señor of much power, *dueño* and lord of many things, carried the siblings off to the bottom of the hill. He gave them the ability to live there with him.

"You are going to have your *suerte,* Gabriel," the señor said. They entered a well-adorned room where there were many flowers. Within the special room there were three gourd jars plugged with corncobs.

The señor of enchantment said to Gabriel, "Grab a jar and open it."

Gabriel grabbed a jar and unplugged it. From inside the jar a white cloud that did not end began to come out. Then the sky was covered completely with clouds. The señor said, "Go rise up in the clouds, carry with you the gourd jar, and make it rain over the southern area for a period of three days."

"Very well," said Gabriel, and he was on the clouds, carrying the jar. When he arrived on the southern coast, he turned the jar mouth down, and a great rain began. Big storms were heard.

After making it rain for three days, Gabriel was returned on the clouds to the hill from which he had departed. He entered the room and put the jar in its place, and the clouds began to go inside the jar, great amounts of clouds. Then he again plugged the jar. That is why after the rains the clouds are returned to the hills—in order to be saved.

Immediately the señor of white hair and a thick, white beard called Miguel and said, "Grab a gourd jar and unplug it."

Well, Miguel grabbed a jar and unplugged it. From within the jar began to flow large quantities of cold. The *dueño* of enchantment said, "Go rise up and dump a strong cold on the earth over the east."

"Fine," said Miguel, and he was elevated by the same force of the cold that came out of the jar.

When he arrived in the east, he turned the face of the jar down, and it began to dump a strong cold on the earth. The people, animals, and plants almost died of the sheer cold. After three days, Miguel returned to the hill and put the jar in its place. It was filled again with the cold, and he plugged it again with the corncob.

The señor of enchantment said, "You, Lorenzo, grab the third gourd jar and unplug it. In accordance with your dream, what it has is your work."

"Very well," said Lorenzo.

He grabbed the last gourd jar and unplugged it. From within the jar, a current of air began to come out that moved the flowers in the room.

The señor of white hair and a thick, white beard said, "Lorenzo, now I command you to go to the north of the earth and make a strong wind for ten days to help the poor people who work under the sun. They need your help. Rise up!"

"Fine," said Lorenzo. He rose up on the same force of the wind, carrying the jar in his right hand, passing over the lakes, mountains, plains, and seas and over the big cities until arriving to the north. There he began to spew out a strong wind over the earth.

The campesinos were very grateful, as were the masons, the quarry workers—all those who work under the sun. Even the animals were appreciative, because the force of the sun was too strong. But the wind came and eased everything.

This is the story of the señora and her three children, a tale of a Tzutuhil of San José la Laguna.

Ignacio Bizarro Ujpán

The Gold and
Silver Fish
Long, long ago in San José lived a really poor family. It was difficult for them to live each day because they could earn scarcely enough for food. The señor sold firewood and mushrooms. The work of his wife was washing clothes for the people of the town. Every day she went down to the shore of the lake. For this they gave her some *reales* [money] and some tortillas.

With *suerte* [luck], they found a *comadre* [co-mother, godmother] and *compadre* [co-father, godfather] who were rich in many things—corn, beans, chickens, sheep, goats, and a lot of money. But they were selfish and miserable. One time the poor *compadre* and his wife headed to the house of the rich *compadres* to ask them for some ideas or advice as to how to get out of their difficult situation. When they arrived, they greeted [the rich *compadres*], saying, "Good evening, *compadre;* good evening, *comadre.*"

The rich *compadres* answered, "*Compadres,* good evening." The poor *compadres* remained standing. The rich *compadres* didn't even offer them chairs in order to sit down a little. Then the rich *compadre* asked them what they wanted, because he didn't have time to chat.

Then the poor *compadres* explained their situation:

Compadre and *comadre,* we have come here to you so that you can give us some advice on how to get out of our difficult circumstance. We are very poor; we don't have anything. Scarcely can we get through each day.

Compadre, comadre, we want some ideas about what you did to get what you have. You have many things and are enjoying your life. We want to get out of the fatal poverty that we are suffering in this desolate life.

Then the rich [*compadre*] and his wife answered at the same time, "We don't have any ideas or advice. We have a lot of things in abundance because we work a lot. We are not lazy and arrogant as you are. You don't have anything to eat because you are arrogant and don't work. You go to bed early and get up late."

This was all the advice that the rich *compadres* gave them. The poor *compadre* and his wife left very sad. The story says that on the road they began to cry, praying to God that he would liberate them from such bitter poverty. Their hope was that soon they would obtain a better life than their rich *compadres.* The poor [*compadre*] still continued selling firewood and mushrooms to the people of the town. Often he didn't sell anything because most of the people of the town had lots of things to eat. His wife always had the same work, washing clothes of the people of the town. But she didn't earn more than a few *reales* and a few tortillas. Every day the señora went down to the shore of the lake very early, at sunrise.

The story says that when she arrived on the shore, she meditated and made the sign of the cross in front of her with her face to the east. She invoked the goddess of the lake, requesting that some day they would be set free from the bitterness of life. So she spent every day, meditating and invoking the goddess of the lake. She did so for a long time.

One day, the story says, the lady went down very early to wash clothing at the edge of the lake. While she was doing the laundry, a kind woman suddenly appeared at her right side. She felt a great fear and almost took off running. But the beautiful señorita said, "Woman, don't be afraid. I won't hurt you. I have come to do you a favor. Tell me everything that is happening to you."

The poor *comadre* answered:

My husband and I are very poor. Every day I come down here to the lake to wash the clothes of the people, and the people give me some *reales* and some tortillas for the clean laundry. This is how I spend my life. But now I feel very tired. My husband sells a little firewood and mushrooms to the people. Our life continues to be a calamity. No one will advise us what to do to live a little better life and be a little happier. We have some *compadres* who are rich. We asked them to help us with some ideas, but they looked unfavorably upon us and treated us as if we were arrogant and lazy. Thus we have not received help from anyone.

The goddess of the lake replied:

I understand your necessity and your poverty. I am the goddess of the lake. Every day I see you on this shore washing, and I always listen to your prayers. The day has arrived. Today you are going to receive a reward for all that you have been suffering. Soon you are going to have gold and silver, and you will have a better life than your *compadres*. Of course, you and your husband are going to have to do many favors for the poor people, and you must not forget the poverty you have seen in life. Don't be miserly or selfish. Don't be envious. Have charity toward your fellow man.

"Very well," said the poor *comadre*, "I will fulfill all your recommendations, and many thanks." Then she dropped to her knee, in order to kiss the hand of the goddess of the lake. When she wanted to grab her hand, in the blink of an eye, she no longer saw anything. The goddess of the lake had disappeared. She was not to be seen. The poor *comadre* remained troubled, wondering what the reward would be. She was very frightened, and she continued washing.

When the rays of the sun were reflecting on the lake, very near the señora appeared a fish, neither very big nor very small. The fish was making many turns very near the poor *comadre*. The woman was amazed by the fish. Every day she had been washing on the edge of the lake and had never seen that fish. But the story says that the fish jumped and fell into the basket of the poor *comadre*. She very happily wrapped the fish in some banana tree leaves and kept it within the basket.

When she finished washing the clothes, she returned to her house. Within the house were two wooden images—the image of Jesús and the image of the Virgen María. The poor *comadre*, very content, put the fish in a small basket and placed it in front of the altar where the two images stood.

She began to prepare a little food for breakfast. When she and her husband were eating, she told him she had obtained a fish on the edge of the lake. When they finished eating, they approached the images. It was extremely strange when they saw that the image of Christ was no longer wooden—it had been changed into gold. Also, the image of the Virgen María was no longer wooden—it had been changed into silver. When the señora grabbed the fish to give it to her husband, it was no longer really a fish. It had been transformed into gold and silver. The story says that one side was gold and the other was silver. The poor *compadre and comadre* fell to their knees and praised God for everything they had received. Also, the story says, they praised the goddess of the lake. Immediately they put the fish of gold and silver in a coffer, and it could be heard clearly when it moved around inside the coffer.

In twenty days they opened the coffer and looked inside. It was full of money. The fish of gold and silver was positioned over the money. The *compadre* and *comadre* were amazed. Not until then were they liberated from the extreme poverty that they had been suffering. They began a better life. They constructed good houses, bought lands, and had money left over. They became the richest persons in town. The townspeople asked one another how they got so much money.

The rich *compadres* were envious of the poor *compadres*, and they looked unfavorably upon them, with much hate. The poor *compadre* and his wife began to help many poor people. They lent money without charging interest, paid the wages of their helpers, bought them land, and sold them corn and beans for a low price.

One day the rich *compadre* said to his wife, "We're going to ask the *compadre* and *comadre* what they did to earn a lot of money. Now they have a lot more than we. Before, they were starving to death and despised. Now they enjoy much prestige." And the rich *compadre* and his wife took to the road until arriving at the house of their *compadres*.

When they arrived, they greeted their *compadres* as usual and immediately told them, "*Compadre, comadre*, we have come here to you so that you may give us an idea. What did you do to obtain so many things? Now you have much more than we."

Then the poor *comadre* answered, saying:

Ay, *compadre, comadre*, we were some poor ones. My husband sold firewood and mush-rooms to the people. My work was washing the clothes of the people, and that's how we earned our food. Now we already have a little of each thing that we needed in the house. But this was *suerte* that the *dueña* [goddess} of the lake gave me when I was wash-ing clothes one morning. The *dueña* of the lake gave me a reward for all the suffering I experienced from doing so much laundry in the lake. Now then, if you want to receive some reward, you will have to be washing clothes for some time. *Comadre*, my recom-pense was that I grabbed a fish, and that fish we kept in a coffer. That was our good fortune, and for that reason, we now have enough money and other things.

"Thank you, *comadre*," said the rich *comadre*. "I will do what's possible. Tomorrow I will begin to wash clothing, although with a little shame. What's important is that the goddess of the lake give me my recompense."

Very contentedly she left with her husband. On the road they were commenting that they were going to have a lot of money. When they arrived in the house, the woman came to an agreement with her husband that she would have to go to the lake to wash the clothing of the people in order to obtain a fortune.

So it was all the mornings. She went down to the shore of the lake in order to wash the clothes of the people. The people of the town were much amazed at that woman, because the truth is that she didn't need to do the laundry of the people. That old woman was very rich and had everything. But her intentions were to have the goddess of the lake give her a reward for so much clothes washing.

A certain morning, the story says, the rich *comadre* was washing on the shore of the lake. A pretty señorita suddenly appeared, singing. Then she spoke to the old woman who was washing clothes and said to her, "Woman, what necessity brings you here to wash clothes of the people, when you have plenty with which to live well?"

She answered the goddess of the lake, saying, "Señora, I am washing clothes as a maid of the people. I, in time, will get my reward, because my poor *comadre* says that is what happened to her. Here, where she was washing clothes for a long time, she grabbed a fish. This was her good fortune. More for that reason, she now lives well with her husband, and they have many things, more than we."

The story says that the goddess of the lake told her, "Woman, continue washing and await the reward of your ambitions. Your fortune is a turtle and a big crab."

The rich *comadre* continued washing very happily, because she was now waiting for her good luck. Without much delay, the story says that out from underneath a rock came a tortoise. She caught it and wrapped it in a banana tree leaf. In a while a very big crab came out. She also caught it and wrapped it in a banana tree leaf. Very happily she put them in her basket.

When she arrived home, she told her husband that she had gotten a double reward on behalf of the goddess of the lake, because she had done nothing less than catch a tortoise and a large crab. She told her husband to go buy two big coffers, one in which to put the turtle and the other in which to put the big crab.

The husband ran to a carpentry shop to buy two very big coffers. When he arrived home, they put the tortoise in one coffer and the crab in the other. They happily were thinking that they were going to gain much money, more than the poor *compadres*.

The story says that they clearly heard the tortoise and the crab when they moved within their coffers. The woman and her husband thought that the tortoise and the crab were working, or making money.

One day the rich *comadre* and *compadre* lifted up the two coffers. They felt as if they now weighed a lot. They said, "Now we already have a lot of money because the coffers already weigh a lot."

In exactly twenty days they said, "Now we are going to open the coffers to see how much money we have." When they opened the first coffer, there was no money, but rather, out from the coffer came innumerable toads and tortoises. It was horrible! And when they opened the second coffer, it was worse—it was full of rattlesnakes and *cantiles* [very poisonous snakes of hot climates *(agkistrodon bilineatus)*].

Out from the coffer came hundreds of snakes. The serpents got in their clothes and jackets. They almost filled up the house. The owners no longer could go in the house from fear of the serpents, tortoises, and toads. The owners of the house were crying a lot and asking for help to kill those dreadful animals.

This happened to them because of their wicked ambitions. Then came to pass what the goddess of the lake had said when she told the woman, "Wait for the reward of your ambitions."

Ignacio Bizarro Ujpán

The Rich and Miserable Man: A Cakchiquel Story

The story says that in a canton of Sololá lived a family. The canton actually is called Canton Tablón [Plank Canton]. The señor—that is, the father of the family—worked a lot during his youth and earned good money. But he had the habit of not eating well or dressing well. His vice was to keep the money that he earned. When the señor got married to his woman, he had plenty of money. It was their luck to have three children.

The father was very bad. He was very cruel to their three children, putting them to work a lot, from very early morning until nightfall.

The señor, the story says, was a miser, not wanting his family to buy a little meat. They ate only tortillas with salt and chili. So they lived their life; he and his family suffered.

The story says that the señor had a charmed power—the money that he had multiplied by itself. One large box was filled and then the other large box was filled. There now were two large boxes—boxes that would hold up to 500 pounds of corn each—that were full of money.

The wife and her three children asked the señor to at least give them a little money to buy a little meat, because they needed to buy a little meat at least once a month. But the señor was a tightwad who did not want to spend a single centavo.

Once, when the señor went to the campo to see how the hired hands were doing with the crops, he took a gourd of water. His wife said, "Better take a little refreshment and a little coffee."

The husband answered, "No, water is better. It doesn't cost money."

Well, the señor went to the field, and the wife and their three children decided to open the large box to take out a little money, taking advantage of the father's absence. When they opened the large box, a big rattlesnake was poised on the money. Who could get inside with that serpent there? It almost bit the señora.

Then they closed the box and opened the other one. In the second locker there were two rattlesnakes—but really big ones. The señora and their children left the other box closed. They didn't succeed in taking out the money that they wanted to spend. They were trembling with fear. It was very strange that within the house were the two large boxes with money, with three big rattlesnakes—two in one box and one in the other.

When the señor arrived home from work, he laid down in his hammock of agave. An hour later he took out a new palm mat and began to expose the money to the sun on the patio of the house. The señora and their children no longer saw the three serpents. They thought that the señor's money was from some enchanted hill.

The señor, the story says, bought good shoes, good clothes, and an expensive Texan hat, but he didn't want to wear them. He wrapped them in a sheet and hung them in a corner of the house.

Always, the señor was of bad character. He didn't love his wife and three children. He liked his two servants more than his family. The servants were the ones in charge of looking after the house, doing the cleaning, and sunning the clothes, the shoes, and the hat of the old man, because if they put them in the sun, the moths would not get in them. They story also says that they were in charge of putting the money in the sun so that it would not get moth-eaten from the humidity.

The children said to their dad, "Better put on your shoes, *papá*. Put on the new clothes, and use the hat. Already you are an old man, and you should enjoy life. What do you want a lot of money for?"

But the father was a miser who didn't want to listen to his children. Over time the señor became old and fell sick.

When he was a few days from dying, he summoned his three children to give them instructions. He told them:

My children, I'm leaving here. I'm dying, my time has arrived. You will remain, but you must do what I tell you. If you don't, you will soon be with me.

Now go to town and buy a box [coffin] for my body, but I want the best box. The cost is not important. There is plenty of money. I want a box like no one else's. When I die and when you come to put me in the box, you must put a lot of money inside the coffin until my body is covered with it, like a blanket of flowers. We live here in a can-ton far from town. When they carry my body, you must buy drinks—many drinks—to give to those who accompany my burial. Since we live far from town, at each crossroad you must rest my body and give plenty to drink to those who accompany it. When you put me in the *panteón* [above-ground tomb], you must give drinks to the people, be they relatives or not, friends or enemies, well-knowns or unknowns. You must give them their drinks until all are drunk, as a remembrance of my existence in this world.

If you do what I tell you, I will go once and for all. You should spend all the money, because the money is mine. All of it will serve for my funeral. But if you don't do what I order, I will come back for you.

On a certain day the señor died. The children bought a very simple wooden mortuary box and prepared for the burial of their father. They put the body within the box, but they didn't cover it with money as he had instructed. The children planned to keep all the money. They did not buy drinks, not even a soda, to give to the visitors or to those who accompanied the deceased in the funeral procession. It was a simple burial—they scarcely spent more than the cost of the mortuary box.

The three children kept most of the inheritance. They allotted the money, the lands, and other things without taking into account the mother. To their mother they gave hardly anything. The three children now felt like the richest people in the canton, because they took possession of all the goods of their deceased father.

It is the custom among us Indians that nine days after the death of a person, one makes a visit to the cemetery, carrying candles, incense, and many flowers to place on the grave or *panteón*. The story says that this is what the children of the deceased intended to do. They invited family and friends to accompany them to the visit the cemetery, but this visit had to be completed before sunset. So the children, relatives, and friends left the canton at four in the morning because the distance was a bit far.

At five in the morning, on the road leading to the town, they passed through the Xolbé canton. When they were passing under some cypress groves, the señor who had been dead for nine days was stationed there; that is, the father of the three hombres was there. They didn't recognize that he was their dad. They were mindful of their father's death nine days previously.

But the story says that the dead man spoke to his three sons, saying, "Julio, Chepe, Pascual, what are you going to do at the cemetery? You have been disobedient. You didn't put the money in the coffin as I said. You didn't buy the drinks as I ordered, and you bought only a cheap coffin. You make use of my money and of my goods. Now I have come for you, and you will see what happens to those who are disobedient."

He then pulled the ears of his three children. They trembled with fear. Other people were like mutes who could not speak because they knew that hombre had already died.

After pulling his three children by the ears, he waved good-bye to the people, and then he disappeared under the cypress groves. They saw him no more.

Now the children no longer wanted to make the visit to the cemetery. They returned to their house very frightened. They could hardly speak.

It is said that they came down with vomiting and diarrhea because a dead person had appeared to them. This was a great fright for the rest of the cantons of Sololá.

Finally, the story says, in three days Julio died, in six days Pascual died, and in nine days Chepe died—all simply from vomiting and diarrhea. And that's how the lives of the three disobedient sons ended.[54]

Domingo Puac of Sololá

The Grandfather and
the Faultfinders

Once, the wife and daughter of a grandfather died, but his daughter left a son named Chito. The two—the grandfather and the grandson, Chito—remained living in the house, but they needed to search for business. Their job was selling charcoal. Every day they went barefoot to the town to sell. Neither had *caites* [open-toed sandals] because the two were Indians. They could speak little Spanish. Some words they understood; other words they didn't.

One day they passed by a bridge where a group of women were washing. The women, seeing the grandfather and grandson each carrying a big load of charcoal, began to judge, saying, "Ay, what a wretched old man. He has the boy under such a heavy load. Well, he is old, but it would be better for him to carry this load, not the boy. The boy should be treated well. What a despicable old man!"

The grandfather said to his grandson, Chito, "Don't pay any attention to those people. They don't have a need as we do. Let's keep on going."

The next day, in order to see what the people would say, only the grandfather carried a big load of charcoal. The grandson didn't carry anything. When they entered the town, there were some señores standing around.

The men began to opine, saying, "Ay, what an unfortunate old man. He bears the load, and the boy carries hardly a thing. It would be better that the boy carry that load, not the old man. He deserves more respect. The boy is young and needs to help the old fellow." Because these people were never satisfied, the grandfather and the grandson became very sad.

One Saturday they went again to town to sell charcoal. Then the grandfather said to his grandson, "Chito, now you carry the load. I will go with you to see what the people will say."

Well, the grandson carried the load of charcoal, and the two went walking. When they passed by a soccer field, they met some young people who were sitting down. Seeing the boy carrying the big load of charcoal and the old man carrying nothing, the young people began to judge, saying, "Ay, that old man has no shame. He is carrying nothing while the boy is collapsing under such a heavy load. A growing boy should not be treated that way. He is innocent, and he doesn't have the strength. On the other hand, that damned old man has a lot of strength. Who knows how much of his life he owes to the boy?"

The grandfather and grandson became very sad, almost crying because the people didn't agree with what they were doing. Then they thought about it and said, "Let's do what suits us, without paying any attention to those who laugh at us."

Every day they entered the town barefoot. A lady came up to the grandfather and said, "Señor, every day I see you passing through here, carrying your charcoal. You two walk a lot. I pity that neither of you can buy a pair of *caites* for your feet."

The grandfather answered, "Thank you for the advice, my very dear señora. That is what we are going to do. We are going to buy ourselves some *caites*." But since they didn't earn much, they thought it would be better first to buy a pair of sandals for the grandfather and then later to buy a pair for the grandson, Chito.

Then one day they went to town, each one carrying his load of charcoal. Before entering the town, they passed near a group of people eating lunch on the side of the road. Seeing that the old grandfather wore *caites* and the boy went barefoot, the people having lunch began to murmur, "Ay, what an old man with a wrinkled face. He is not only old, but he also wears *caites,* while the boy goes barefoot. It would be better that the boy wear the sandals. He is a boy with very tender feet. The old man is the one who should be barefoot."

Under the load of charcoal, tears now were falling from the eyes of the grandfather. He said to his grandson, "Chito, this world is hell. It's full of judges and mockers. The people are not in favor of whatever we do. They are judging us badly for everything. But, God willing, tomorrow will be a better day."

The next day, very early, they prepared their bundles of charcoal. The grandfather told his grandson, "You, Chito, my good grandson, you have to wear the sandals. Let's see what the people will say about us now. I hope now they won't mock us."

Well, they carried their charcoal. The young lad was wearing the *caites,* and the grandfather wore nothing [on his feet].

On the road they met a priest. They greeted him and even kissed his hand. The priest said to the young boy, "You are sinning against heaven and against your father. The law says to honor your father and mother, so that you will live a better life on earth. It is appropriate that your father wear the sandals. He is an old man who has endured much suffering. But you are a young boy whose life is ahead of you. You will find your fortune on earth."

The young man answered the priest, "Señor priest, you tell me that the law says to honor my father and mother, but they have died already. The señor with whom I'm living is my grandfather. It suits him that I put on the *caites*. The Bible says, 'Blessed are the children, for theirs is the kingdom of heaven.'"

The unfortunate priest gave up and did not respond further. He said good-bye very sadly and pensively.

On the road the grandfather and the grandson began discussing their situation.

They concluded that neither of them would wear the *caites*. They threw them in a ravine so that the people of this world would be happy.

The grandfather and grandson continued to sell charcoal. Over time, their hair fell out from the wear of the porter's strap. They were bald. Both of them now looked like grandfathers.

One day a señora shopping in the market spoke to the grandfather: "Señor, I pity you. Using the porter's strap so much has caused you to lose your hair. But I'm going to give you a piece of advice that will serve you well—buy a little donkey to help you carry the cargo!"

The grandfather was very grateful for the señora's advice. It was true that he and his grandson were tired of carrying such heavy loads every day.

That's the way it was. They saved some money and bought a little donkey. When they had the donkey, they threw the load on it and followed behind, carrying nothing. The people of the town began to opine, saying, "Ay, what brutish people! Those two carry nothing while the poor donkey nearly collapses under the load. These two hairless ones should not be given food for a week."

The grandfather said to his grandson, "Chito, the people are never satisfied. They are judging us very wrongly. But tomorrow is another day. Let's see what the people say tomorrow."

The next day after selling charcoal, when they were returning home, the grandfather said to his grandson, "I'm going to mount the little burro. Because of my age, I'm already feeling tired. I'm old. But tomorrow you will ride the donkey."

"Very well, grandfather," said Chito.

The grandfather went mounted on the donkey, and Chito walked. They passed by some nuns. When the sisters saw that the old man was mounted on the donkey and the boy was walking, they said, "There goes that old, sandal-faced, bald-headed rascal. He has no shame, riding a donkey while the boy suffers, walking on foot. It would be more appropriate for the boy to ride the donkey and not that rickety old man."

Without recourse, the grandfather began to cry from what he heard every day. Each day the ridicule saddened him more.

The next day, after selling the charcoal, when they were returning home, the grandfather said to his grandson, "Now, Chito, you need to ride on the little burro. Yesterday the nuns made fun of me when I rode the animal."

"Very well, grandfather," said Chito, and he mounted the donkey. Very calmly they headed for the road.

While they were walking, they met an evangelist pastor, who said to the boy:

My dear brother, have some consideration. Get off the burro. It is not suitable for you to ride it. You are a young lad. It's better that your grandfather ride it. He deserves respect. He is very old, and he has experienced a lot of things in life. In contrast, you are young and still growing. You have a lot ahead of you. You can expect a lot from God. You should go on foot, and your grandfather should ride the donkey.

Chito answered the pastor:

Señor, I don't understand the kind of people who live in this world. Yesterday my grandfather was riding the burro. Some nuns made fun of him, saying that he is a wretched, rickety old man and that it isn't suitable for him to ride the burro. The sisters said it would be better for me to ride the burro. Now you say that my grandfather should ride it. I want to know which of us you value more, my grandfather or me? Perhaps I'm not worth anything. You are all faultfinders. We have been suffering by the mouths of people for a long time. I want to know the truth. Which of us do you value more?

The pastor responded, "My dear brother, your grandfather deserves respect, but by the law of humanity and of God, the two of you are of equal worth."

"Thank you, dear pastor. If the two of us are of equal worth, then it is suitable for both of us to ride on the burro." Then the two mounted the donkey and went riding off, while the poor pastor was left standing in the road.

When they were passing in front of the church of the town, thereabouts was standing a priest, whose soul was shaken, seeing that the two were mounted on the donkey and that the poor animal was suffering.

The priest spoke: "Don't be so brutish. You are going to kill the poor animal. The two of you can't ride him at the same time. Don't be savages!"

The grandfather and grandson got down off the burro and told the priest, "Señor priest, we are really tired of so much ridicule. The mouths of the people are [too confining], like a tomb. We don't want them to judge us anymore. Señor priest, we give you our burro and hope that he will assist you."

They continued walking and walking. Who knows where they are now? What is known is that the little donkey lives with the priest and serves him well in the rural areas where there still are no highways. The priest goes to those places mounted on a burro.

Colorín colorado, this story is finished.

Ignacio Bizarro Ujpán

The Nuns and the
Charcoal Vendor

It is said that when young ladies are studying to become nuns, they are well chaperoned by their teachers. They are not allowed to go out on trips—not even on the streets to run errands—so that they do not become familiar with the sins of the people; that is, so they do not see drunks, women with many children, and, of course, prostitutes.

One day a poor charcoal vendor arrived in the city to sell his charcoal. But in order to sell his charcoal, the poor man had to offer it to people who needed it.

It is said that in this city there was a nunnery. The charcoal salesman left his burro tied up in front of the church near the nunnery. But he was having a hard day because people were not buying his charcoal, and he spent a lot of time offering it to various individuals.

This is what was happening when the nuns and their teacher decided to take a small excursion around the church, so that they could get some fresh air.

Then the nuns went very happily for a walk, looking at the birds and the butterflies in the garden. They asked the mother superior the names of the birds, the butterflies, and the flowers. The mother superior happily told them the names of all these things. They were doing this when they came to where the charcoal merchant's donkey was tied up. The nuns were very pleased when they saw the animal. They gathered round, forming a circle, and asked the teacher what the name of this animal was. They were surprised because they had never seen a jackass.

Then the mother superior told them, "This is a burro. It belongs to some provincial who sells charcoal." The nuns did not want to continue their walk because they enjoyed looking at the charcoal dealer's burro.

It is said that the donkey became aware that the nuns were very pleased with him. Who knows what the jackass felt, but suddenly his member (penis) stood up, and the nuns shouted with glee when they saw his erect member. They asked the teacher, "What is the name of this thing that the burro has?"

The mother superior became angry and did not want to answer their question. She wanted to take the nuns inside and confine them immediately, but they did not want to go. They were laughing when the donkey moved his member. It is said they insisted on asking, "What is the name of this thing that the burro has?"

And the mother superior angrily answered, "I do not know about this burro's penis."

Then the student nuns said, "Then the name of it is a penis."

The mother superior very angrily went to look for a policeman to come and take the animal away from the area of the church. The policeman, pretending to be preoccupied, went through the streets looking for the owner of the burro. Because of the policeman's good luck, he came upon a man smoking a cigarette, and he asked him, "Could that burro that is in front of the church be yours?"

The charcoal peddler said, "Yes, señor policeman, the burro is mine. It's that I'm prolonging my time here, offering my charcoal to the people who do not want to pay the price I am asking."

The policeman said, "Please remove your burro from the front of the church because the mother superior is very angry. That burro has an erect penis, and she does not want the nuns to see it."

"Very well, jefe, I will go take him away right now," said the charcoal seller. When he arrived at the place where he had left his donkey, it is said the nuns were dying of laughter, opening and closing their eyes. When the owner gave a jolt to the donkey's member with his cigarette, the donkey's organ then shrank.

The nuns said, "What happened to its member? What a shame!" they said, and they left very sadly.

But it is said that the policeman was curious about what the owner had done to make the jackass lose his erectness. The policeman, a smile on his face, said, "Amigo charcoal vendor, what did you say to the burro, because when you arrived he put away his member?"

The charcoal vendor said, "No, jefe, I cannot say. Only I know how to talk to my burro."

The policeman, upset, said, "Tell me, and when you leave the burro again in the area of the church, I will say the same thing to him so that the teacher of the nuns will not get angry."

The charcoal salesman answered, "But if I tell you, you might get angry and imprison me for the rest of my life."

The policeman told him, "Under no circumstances will I get upset or angry, much less put you in jail. You will be doing me a favor, because with the time I have left to serve, I will know many things."

"Very well, jefe, this is what I said to my burro. 'Burro of mine, put away your penis because the policeman might eat it. It's that the police are very quick because they do not earn enough. They even will eat the member of a burro.'"

It is said that when the policeman heard these things, he became very angry, but he had promised to do no harm to the charcoal merchant. The charcoal vendor, however, had not actually said these things, but rather he had burned the donkey with his cigarette.

Colorín colorado, this tale has ended, and what a delicious meal was offered to the *polaco* [cop].

Ignacio Bizarro Ujpán

Notes

1. This project, which lasted from 1969 to 1975 and was directed primarily by Clyde, generated several master's theses and doctoral dissertations at UCLA. Members of the 1970–72 crews who collected both qualitative and quantitative data for the project included Sandra Orellana, now professor and chair of anthropology, California State University, Dominguez; José (Benny) Cuellar, professor and chair of La Raza studies, San Francisco State University; M. L. (Tony) Miranda, professor of anthropology, University of Nevada, Las Vegas; Margo-Lea Hurwicz, associate professor of anthropology, University of Missouri, Saint Louis; James Diego Vigil, professor of anthropology and Chicano(a) studies and director of the Center for the Study of Urban Poverty at UCLA; Douglas Sharon, director, San Diego Museum of Man; and myself, Regents' Professor of Anthropology, Northern Arizona University.

Clyde Woods and I have published a number of articles and books that analyze both the quantitative and the qualitative data collected from this project. These include Sexton (1972, 1978, 1979a, 1979b), Woods (1975), and Sexton and Woods (1977, 1982).

2. Alfredo Herbruger Jr. and Eduardo Díaz Barrios (1956:66) believe that the Cakchiqueles might have named the town of Sololá after this nearby waterfall since *Sololá* means "splashed water" *(agua suplicada)* or "waterfall" *(catarata de agua)*.

3. Current anthropological theory states that the forebearers of all American Indians entered the Americas in separate waves from North Asia via a land bridge through the Bering Strait between 40,000 and 100,000 years ago (Birdsell 1951; Carmack et al. 1997:42; Boyd 1998). Contemporary biological studies indicate that American Indians share many genetic characteristics with Asian peoples. In a number of ways, however, American Indians have external features that differ from those of Asians: they have high frequencies of the convex nose and of blood Type O but, except for the Eskimos, a general absence of blood Type B and of the epicanthic fold that are found among Asians. These differences suggest that American Indians have long been separated from their relatives in Asia (Birdsell 1972:435; Carmack et al. 1997:20).

4. In this introduction I am using the real names of towns unless otherwise indicated. In the text of the folktales and their accompanying notes, I have changed some of the names of the towns and the people to protect their privacy.

5. During the second half of the 1995 sabbatical, I traveled with my wife, Marilyn,

129

to Peru, Bolivia, Ecuador, and Colombia to collect firsthand information for the course I teach on the peoples of Latin America.

6. All of the tales that Ignacio gave to me he had written in Spanish. When he used Tzutuhil Mayan words, he provided the Spanish equivalents in parentheses. In these instances, I have retained his Mayan expressions in italics and provided English translations—rather than his Spanish ones—in parentheses. For example, when Ignacio wrote "*itz'el tak' winak ('demonios,' los españoles),*" I translated *itz'el tak' winak* ("demons," the Spaniards). Definitions or other interpolations enclosed in brackets are my own.

Also, I have used a free style of translation to reach a wider audience than would be possible with a literal translation, which would be of interest mainly to Mayan scholars. Thus I have made verb tenses in a paragraph consistent, made the subject and verb in a sentence agree in number, and deleted most of the repetitions that are typically found in Mayan folktales.

Throughout the tales, when I have retained a Mayan or Spanish word or expression in the text, I have italicized it and provided a definition in English in parentheses or brackets, as explained above. To help the general reader, these definitions appear upon the first usage of each term in each tale. They also appear in a glossary at the end of the book.

If an Indian or Spanish word (such as *jefe*) appears in *Merriam Webster's Collegiate Dictionary,* I did not italicize or define it. Some readers may be surprised at the number of such words that have been incorporated into English as loan words.

With the exception of "Heart of Heaven, Heart of Earth" and "The Nuns and the Charcoal Vendor," which I have placed first and last in the collection, the tales appear in random order; that is, in nearly the same order I received them. Like Robert Laughlin and Carol Karasik (1988), I have not regrouped the stories into special categories such as animal tales, creation tales, legends, or tales of supernatural powers.

7. One would address a letter to a person living in the town and department of Sololá as "Sololá, Sololá," just as one would address a letter to a person living in the city and state of New York as "New York, New York."

8. The Tzutuhil towns of Santa María Visitación, San Juan la Laguna, San Pablo la Laguna, and San Pedro la Laguna are on the western side of the lake. Santiago Atitlán, another Tzutuhil town, is to the southwest of the lake, while its *aldea,* Cerro de Oro, is to the southeast. Cerro de Oro was originally settled by Cakchiquel speakers from Patzicía (east of the old highway to Guatemala City), but the majority of the townspeople now speak Tzutuhil. The Tzutuhil town of San Lucas Tolimán, which is on the southeastern shore of the lake, has a sizable number of Cakchiquel speakers.

The Cakchiquel towns of San Antonio Palopó, Santa Catarina Palopó, Panajachel, San Andrés Semetabaj, Sololá, and San Jorge la Laguna (actually, an *aldea* of Sololá) are to the east and northeast of the lake. Santa Cruz la Laguna, another Cakchiquel town, is to the north, and the Cakchiquel town of San Marcos la Laguna is to the northwest.

The Quiché town of Santa Clara la Laguna is to the west of the lakeshore on an elevated plateau high in the mountains. Santa Lucía Utatlán, another Quiché town, is also in the mountains to the northwest, fairly distant from the lakeshore. Quiché is also spoken in and around Santa María Visitación (Sexton and Woods n.d.; Dayley 1985).

For consistency with my previous publications and the vast majority of the literature on Guatemala, I have retained the traditional spelling of Indian proper names. As Dennis Tedlock (1996:202) mentions, these spellings are the ones most commonly followed in Spanish and English publications, although a bewildering number of spellings exists in the literature. One of the most frequent problems readers have with this literature is gaining a command of the Indian words that appear in the texts.

9. Many authors, not all of them linguists, have provided different language classifications in Mesoamerica in general and Guatemala in particular. In colloquial English, the terms "dialect" and "language" may be used interchangeably, but linguists point out that any linguistic classification is somewhat subjective. In the clear-cut cases, languages are mutually unintelligible and dialects are divisions that are found within languages and are mutually intelligible (Justeson and Broadwell 1997:379). Not all cases are clear-cut, however. For example, Oxlajuuj Keej (in England 1996:187), in reference to the classification of languages in Guatemala, states, "There are a number of Mayan languages that are mutually intelligible."

In some cases, linguistic classification has as much to do with politics as with scholarship. If a classifier believes an ethnic group should be identified as a separate culture or subculture, he or she may be inclined to be a linguistic splitter rather than a lumper. The current debate over ebonics (McKinley 1996), or black English, in the United States is a good example of the political nature of linguistic classification.

Nora England (1996:191–192) provides another example from a Guatemalan context. She mentions a dispute regarding the status of Achi, a dialect of Quiché (K'iche' [England et al. 1993] or K'ichee' [England 1996]), in which a linguist in the Achi community wishes to classify Achi as Quiché whereas other members of the community wish to keep it separate to assert their distinct political identity. In the introduction to the volume to which England contributed her article, Edward Fischer and McKenna Brown (1996:9) state, "The country's Maya population comprises twenty-one separate language groups concentrated in the western highlands (map 2)," and on the map they name nineteen of the twenty-one language groups, including Achi. In contrast, England (1996:178) lumps Achi into Quiché and says, "There are twenty Mayan languages spoken in Guatemala." In the same volume, Demetrio Cojtí Cuxil (1996:36) says there are "twenty-three subordinated linguistic communities."

In *Mayan Folktales* (Sexton 1992b), I gave the language classification for Guatemala found in *Geografía Visualizada* by Julio Piedra Santa A., a Guatemalan teacher and author. In the most recent revision of this booklet (1994), the classification is the same, with six groups of the Maya-Quiché (Mayance) family plus the Caribe group and with the traditional orthography. The groups are the following: (1) Quiché (Quiché, Cakchiquel, Tzutujil, and Uspanteca); (2) Mam (Mam, Aguacateca, Jacalteca, Kanjobal, Chuj, and Ixil); (3) Pocomam (Kekchí, Pocomchí, Eastern Pocomam, and Central Pocomam); (4) Chol (Chortí and Chol Lacandón); (5) Maya (Northern Lacandón, Yucateco, and Mopán); and (6) Caribe (Araguaco Caribe, and Spanish Kekchí).

Piedra Santa's classification is similar to those of Herbruger and Díaz Barrios (1956:61–63) and Terrence Kaufman (1974:1). Kaufman, a linguist whose classification scheme is a standard reference in Mesoamerican studies, states that there is a Mayance family but that its groups are Yucateco, Chol, Kanjobal, Mam, Quiché, and Huasteco (in Mexico).

Robert C. West and John P. Augelli (1966:390; 1989:390–391), cultural geographers rather than linguists, identify the family as Mayance, or Maya-Quiché, but they use somewhat different groups: Quiché, Mam, Pocomam, Chol, Chontal, and Tzeltal-Tzotzil, the latter two in Mexico. They say that there are some twenty-three different Mayance languages spoken in Guatemala. Similarly, P. A. Kluck (1983:52) states, "Guatemala's

Indians are Mayans belonging to an estimated 18 to 28 linguistically distinct groups. The principal dialects are Quiché, Cakchiquel, Kekchi, and Mam."

The Carib group, the only language identified as non-Mayance, is unique. Ilah Fleming (1966:303) writes that Central American Carib is a language spoken along the Caribbean coastal areas of Honduras, Guatemala, and Belize. Speakers of this language are blacks who are sometimes called *morenos.*

In 1797 a group of about 5,000 blacks was deported to the coast of Honduras by the British in an effort to end troublesome rebellions in the Lesser Antilles island of Saint Vincent. The deportees represented an aggressive group that had developed from freed and escaped slaves who had sought refuge among the Island Carib Indians during the seventeenth and eighteenth centuries. These Africans, probably of different tribal and linguistic backgrounds, united and became known as the Black Caribs. In contrast to the Island Carib Indians, who today are an almost nonexistent cultural group, the Black Caribs are now a growing group.

The Central American Carib language is a member of the South American Arawakan language family. According to Fleming, however, the speech of male Caribs differs from that of their female counterparts. During a pre-Columbian attack on the Arawak Indians, a group of Carib Indians killed the Arawak men and took many of the women as their wives. Over time, both their male and their female descendants used Arawakan grammar, but the men also attempted to teach their male offspring Carib words to reinforce their status as males. As a result, men used more Carib words and women more Arawakan words. According to John Justeson and George Broadwell (1997:383), many linguists believe that for a period of time there were distinct men's and women's languages on Saint Vincent, but the women's Arawakan language, which is now called Garífuna, was the one that survived, and the people continued to be called Caribs.

For highland Guatemala, Sol Tax (1946, 1968) has cautioned against drawing erroneous conclusions about subcultures and dialects, arguing more for town subcultures of lakeshore towns. That is, Tax claimed that there is little social and political unity among the various Indian groups and that the *municipio* (municipal district, town) is the most important unit binding people who are often related by blood, local customs, and dialect.

Relying on the research of Manuel Andrade (1946), a linguist at the University of Chicago, Tax (1946:5) concluded that even towns whose residents speak the same dialect of one language may show differences in phonetics, vocabulary, and grammar. This is the case for San Juan and San Pedro, which have the same dialect of Tzutuhil, and for San Antonio and Santa Catarina, which have the same dialect of Cakchiquel. That is, there are slight differences of speech between people speaking the same language but living in different towns, or dialectical differences based on towns or location. But Tax (1946:5, 1968:28) also stated, "The Tzutuhil and Cakchiquel of the towns of the lake are very close, so close that no linguist would consider them more than dialects of one language." With the exception of Santiago Atitlán, the Indians of any town can get along in conversation with those of any other town. The people of Santiago Atitlán have a tendency to talk so fast and to raise their voices so extraordinarily high that native speakers in towns farther away can't understand them. Like the academics who study them, the people themselves vary with respect to which languages and dialects they consider to be mutually intelligible.

The most recent linguistic classification for Guatemala is that of England et al. (1993:5), who identified twenty Mayan languages written in the unified alphabet for the

Academia de las Lenguas Mayas de Guatemala (Academy of Mayan Languages of Guatemala). This alphabet was "legalized" by presidential decree in 1987 (England 1996:183) and ratified by the Guatemalan Congress in 1990 (Perera 1993:335). It is now known as the "official" alphabet for Mayan languages in Guatemala but not, as far as I know, in countries such as Mexico, Honduras, and Belize that also have Mayan speakers. The following is the classification scheme of England et al., including (in parentheses) the earlier equivalents of spelling for the twenty Mayan languages of Guatemala: (1) Akateko (Acateco), (2) Awakateko (Aguacateco), (3) Ch'orti' (Chortí), (4) Chuj (Chuj), (5) Itzaj (Itzá), (6) Ixil (Ixil), (7) Kaqchikel (Cakchiquel), (8) K'iche' (Quiché), (9) Mam (Mam), (10) Mopan (Mopán), (11) Popti' (Jacalteco), (12) Poqomchi' (Pocomchí), (13) Poqomam (Pocomam), (14) Q'anjob'al (Kanjobal), (15) Q'eqchi' (Kekchí), (16) Sakapulteko (Sacapulteco), (17) Sipakapense (Sipacapense), (18) Teko (Teco, Tectiteco), (19) Tz'utujiil (Tzutujil, Tzutuhil), and (20) Uspanteko (Uspanteco).

10. In the literature on Middle America (Central America and Mexico), the term *nagual* (also spelled *nahual*) has a number of different meanings, depending on the author and the location under discussion. As Benson Saler (1964:306) points out, *nagual* generally has two meanings: (1) a companion or guardian spirit and (2) a transforming witch. In the Lake Atitlán area, it usually refers to the animal form of a person, especially a *brujo*, who may cause harm to someone, or to the human who is able to transform himself or herself into an animal. Less often it may be referred to as a person's spiritual form. In the *Title of the Lords of Totonicapán*—which was written in Quiché, apparently in 1554; translated into Spanish by Father Dionisio José Chonay; and then translated into English by Delia Goetz—there is mention of *naguales*. Goetz (1953:169) writes, "The *nahuales* were the guardian spirits of the Indians; but here the word has the meaning 'prudent men.' Further on, the gods of the tribes are called *nahuales*." In *Calendario Maya: El camino infinito del tiempo*, Marco and Marcus de Paz (1991:35) seem to be influenced by the *Title of the Lords of Totonicapán* in discussing the significance of the twenty day-names of the Mayan calendar, for they say, "Each one of the 20 days has its *Nahual* or its *dueño*, who exercised influence over the persons that were born on the said day." Other authors refer to these deities as day-lords (Tedlock 1992:106) or day-gods (Colby and Colby 1981:231). Ronald Wright (1991:246) learned the names of the twenty days from an elderly man in Acul, an Ixil town. In front of the names, his informant put the title *Kub'all*, which in the Ixil language is the word for God, lord, or father.

In the Lake Atitlán region, a *dueño* is the owner, master, lord, or god of a locale. In discussing the Q'eqchi (formerly spelled Kekchí) region of Guatemala, Richard Wilson (1995:53–54) refers instead to telluric deities or to local mountain spirits called *tzuultaq'as*. "The tzuultaq'as are spirits that have human form and live in a 'house,' the cave, deep inside the mountain. . . . Only one tzuultaq'a resides in each mountain; it is called the owner of that mountain."

In the famous Viking Fund seminar on Middle America, Charles Wisdom (1968:122) acknowledges the problem in precisely defining the term *nagual* when he says that the *nagual* of an individual, half spirit and half real, attaches itself to a person at birth and protects him throughout his life but that this concept is only imperfectly understood by the present-day Indians. A person may discover the identity of his *nagual* by spreading ashes to examine the footprints it leaves behind. The identity of the *nagual*, he adds, may also be discovered through divination. According to Wisdom, "Nagualism has by now got confused with the animal transformation of sorcerers and witches." George

Foster (1968:137) thinks that Wisdom mixes up two concepts, stating that in some parts of Middle America, such as Chiapas, the *nagual* is the guardian or associated spirit animal. Elsewhere, according to Foster, the *nagual* is a witch that transforms himself into an animal known in Guatemala as a *characotel*. "What we've got here," he says, "is the associated or guardian spirit linked with the spirit of the dead."

Richard Adams and Arthur Rubel (1969:336) state that there are three different spirits that play a role in illness and curing in Guatemalan culture: the *nagual*, the *tonal*, and the soul. To them, *nagual* refers to the special transformation of a man into an animal; the term helps define a witch, who plays a role in making someone sick. The *tonal* is a companion animal or destiny. The soul, mainly a Christian concept, is a shadow or ghost. Both the *tonal* and the shadow soul are subject to theft, which can make someone ill.

In Carlos Castaneda's popular books (1968, 1971, 1972, 1974), there is much discussion by Don Juan, a shaman, and Castaneda, his apprentice, about the significance of the *tonal* and the *nagual*, although their definitions vary from most of the usages found in the literature on Middle America, which in part has caused some critics to claim Castaneda's writing is fiction. Nevertheless, Douglas Sharon (1978:144–145) discusses how the terms can be used to clarify the symbol system of Eduardo, a Peruvian shaman to whom he served as an apprentice. In *Tales of Power*, as Sharon points out, Castaneda reports on the meaning of the *tonal* and *nagual*. The two terms refer to the dual nature of everyone, the *tonal* being the social person, giving order and knowledge and acting as one's guardian. The *nagual* is the indescribable side of a person that has no feelings or knowledge.

For the Aztecs, Frances Berdan (1982:145–146) states, the ritual calendar, or *Tonalpohualli*, "was used to divine the fate of individuals, to foresee the fortunes of the empire, and to determine propitious days for the celebrations of major events." Each of the twenty day-names had its own patron deity who gave special qualities to that day. For instance, the patron of the day named for the wind was Quetzalcoatl, who in one of his guises presided over the wind. The patron of the day named after the rabbit was Mayahuel, the goddess of the maguey. People born on rabbit days could expect a life of drunkenness because of Mayahuel's intoxicating nectar. The days of the calendar themselves were considered good, bad, or indifferent depending on the patron gods and the thirteen numbers associated with them.

Sandra Orellana (1987:29) writes that the concepts of *tonal (tonalli*, a Nahua term) and *nagual* have become intertwined. In ancient belief, the *tonalli* was a life force, essential to an individual's constitution, that each person received depending on the day of his or her birth. The main way the *tonalli* could cause illness was to leave the body. Today, in areas of Middle America such as Chiapas, there is an associated belief called the *tona*. When a human is born, a companion animal who lives in a mountain near the person's home is also born. Part of the person's life force is contained in the animal, and the two share a common fate. In highland Guatemala, according to Orellana, belief in the *tona, tonalism*, and *nagualism* have merged, and the distinctions between them are not clear. Thus when Fuentes y Guzmán, writing in the late 1600s about the days of the ritual calendar, listed plants and objects as well as animals as *naguales*, he was really referring to the earlier concept of *tonas*. "This represents a melding of the concept of tona with that of the animals, plants, and objects which appear in the divinatory calendar" (Orellana 1987:33). Whereas *nagual* in ancient Mexico and in present-day highland Guatemala refers to a person with a magical ability to turn into animals (designating either the person or the animal), *tona* refers to the relationship between one person and one animal, plant, or object. And the person does not assume the form of his or her *tona.*

In the Lake Atitlán area, the words *nagual* and *characotel* are used among my Tzutuhil and Cakchiquel informants. None, however, has ever mentioned the concept of the *tona* (or *tonal*).

11. When I first translated this tale in the spring of 1995, I was uncertain whether to render *cay (cielo)* as "sky" or "heaven." In his translation of the *Popol Vuh,* Tedlock (1985:341) translated the corresponding Quiché terms, *U4ux cah, U4ux uleu,* as "Heart of Sky, Heart of Earth." In Delia Goetz and Sylvanus Morley's (1950:82) English translation of Adrián Recinos's Spanish version, however, *cah* is translated as "heaven." In fact the two translations of the *Popol Vuh* are considerably different. For example, a passage translated by Goetz and Morley (1950:82) as, "In this manner the sky existed and also the Heart of Heaven, which is the name of God and thus He is called" is translated by Tedlock (1996:65) as, "And of course there is the sky, and there is also the Heart of Sky. This is the name of the god, as it is spoken." Tedlock (1985:341; 1996:341) goes on to say, "Heart of Sky, sometimes followed by Heart of Earth (which never appears by itself), is an epithet for the god or gods otherwise named Hurricane, New Born Thunderbolt, and Raw Thunderbolt." In the *Popol Wuh,* Albertina Saravia E. (1980:4) adds that there are three manifestations of Hurricane (Hurakan)—Caculha Hurakan, or Lightning with One Leg; Chipi Caculha, or The Smallest of Lightning; and Raxa Caculha, or Very Beautiful Lightning. As Tedlock (1983:264) points out, if Heart of Sky (Heaven) alludes to God, then the three manifestations of Hurricane may allude to the Holy Trinity (the Father, the Son, and the Holy Ghost). Saravia (1980:1–3) also says that Heart of Heaven is the creator and maker, mother and father of everything, and her translation implies that Heart of Heaven, Heart of Earth is the embodiment of one god (Saravia 1980:164–165).

In the summer of 1995 and the winter of 1996, I specifically questioned Ignacio about the translation of the phrase *Ruc'ux Caj, Ruc'ux Uleep.* He said that it refers to two separate gods, one in heaven and one on earth. When I asked him whether he meant to say "sky" or "heaven," he said he meant the latter, the place where God is. When I asked him if this was the same concept as that in the *Popol Vuh,* he said yes. This may explain why Ignacio, fluent in both Quiché and Tzutuhil, wrote in the folktale the Quiché word *uleu,* for "earth," but in our oral conversation repeatedly said the Tzutuhil word *uleep.* In Tzutuhil, *cux* means "heart" or "center," and *ru* is a possessive prefix that means "its, her, or his." As Jon Dayley (1985) points out, in Tzutuhil, body parts often require possessive prefixes, so *Ruc'ux* literally means "its-heart." Tedlock (1985:341) renders a similarly literal translation for the Quiché words *U4ux cah, U4ux uleu* (its-heart sky, its-heart earth). Because Ignacio indicated that *caj* refers to the same place that God resides, I decided to follow Goetz, Morley, and Recinos and translate *cay* as "heaven" rather than "sky," although calling it heaven could simply reflect present-day religious syncretism, equating the Christian god with the pre-Columbian Mayan god.

The Spanish word *cielo* is similar to the Vietnamese word *troi.* In reference to Le Ly Hayslip and Jay Wurts's *When Heaven and Earth Changed Places,* Renny Christopher (1995:324) points out that in Vietnamese *troi* can mean either "heaven" or "sky." For two delightful Vietnamese folktales that refer to heaven and earth, see "The Tea Server from Heaven," and "Rice Cakes for the New Year" in Alice Terada (1989). For more discussion of religious syncretism in the *Popol Vuh,* see Robert Carmack (1981:316–320) and Dennis Tedlock (1983:262–271).

12. The corn for *atol* is cooked with ash from wood fires, just as the corn for tortillas is cooked with lime. Then the *masa* (corn dough) is cooked in large earthenware bowls. Separately, a condiment is made of toasted yellow corn ground with the *piedra de moler,* or arm of the grinding stone. *Aniz* (anise), *chan* (herb whose seeds are small black grains), and a little chili are added to this condiment, which is then mixed in a clay bowl and added to the corn dough to give it a spicy flavor. When it is consumed, the whole product is called *atol.* It is a filling dish that has the texture of Cream of Wheat but is much more tasty.

13. Marco and Marcus de Paz (1991:32–33) provide different meanings for Bakbal and Noj, but this is not surprising; Eric Thompson (1971) and Barbara Tedlock (1992) point out that there is considerable variation in whether a particular shaman considers a given day to be lucky or unlucky, and Tedlock notes that her informants often contradicted themselves. For example, one of her informants stated that a child born on Cawuk (Ignacio's Cauok) is apt to have bad luck, whereas three shamans told Ignacio that it would have good luck. These same shamans also told Ignacio the significance of the other seventeen day-lords, whose names are Ajpub, Aj, Ey, Ix, Batz, Quemel, Tziquin, Imox, K'ik, Tijax, Can, Kjánel, Toj, Ajmac, Kat, Quej, and Tzi.

14. Ignacio provided me with some additional examples of Tzutuhil beliefs and related *secretos:*

> If a person goes out at night to run an errand or for any other purpose and he or she is persecuted by a *characotel* [person similar to a witch who can turn into his or her *nagual* form and do harm to someone], to stop the *characotel* from bothering him or her, the person performs the following *secreto:* he or she takes off his [or her] trousers or slacks and turns them inside out. He or she does the same thing with his shirt or her blouse. They say that the *characotel* then can't recognize whether the person is a man or a woman, and this is the best *secreto.*
>
> When there is a lot of fighting or discord between a married man and woman, to have peace one must do a *secreto.* One must sweep the house and take out all the trash with an old piece of clothing of the man and woman and burn it on the patio of the house in the afternoon in the sunlight. Only in this way is the fighting ended in the home.
>
> If an evil spirit enters to bother the inhabitants of a house, one must perform a *secreto* to repel it. One grabs the broom and strikes four blows with it in each corner of the house and finally on the door. Only in this way does the evil spirit leave, crying.
>
> If an evil spirit pursues a person in the night when he or she is traveling, for this there is a *secreto.* With a machete or with another object, one must dig a hole in the ground and put his or her mouth and nose in it, and then the evil spirit can do no harm.
>
> A pregnant woman cannot go outside at night. She must stay inside the house. If she leaves, the devil will incarnate himself in her, causing a child to be born a *characotel* or *brujo* or with physical defects. To prevent the devil from embodying itself in a pregnant woman, the woman must carry a *secreto* [magical object] when

she goes out at night. She must carry a piece of lit *ocote* [a resinous pine] to keep the devil from harming her unborn child because the devil is afraid of *ocote*.

And, finally, there is the belief that a dead person must be buried with his or her face toward the west. They do this so that the spirit of the deceased goes to rest once and for all. If this isn't done, the dead one's spirit continues bothering (scaring) his wife and children.

On the ninth day after burial, the survivors wash all of the deceased's clothing. Then they whitewash everything where he or she was living, regardless of whether the house is *bajareque* [cane and mud] or adobe. This *secreto* is good for the family because the spirit of the dead forgets where he or she was living when he or she was in this life. In other words, the spirit then does not recognize his or her house because it is white.

15. Predominantly ancient Mayan stories include "Heart of Heaven, Heart of Earth: A Tzutuhil Tale," "Story of the Goddess of the Lake," "A Very Old Story [of Creation]," "The Angels Who Were Eternally Punished for the Evil They Committed on Earth," "Story of an Enchanted Place, Paruchi Abaj," "Story of the Emigration of a Cakchiquel People," "A Sacred Story," "Story of the Owl," and "Doña María and Her Three Children."

More contemporary Mayan stories include "The Story of a Tzutuhil Named Adrián from San Pedro la Laguna," "Story of a Hunter," "The Man Who Wanted to Learn to Be a *Brujo* and a *Characotel*," "The Story of the Assistants Who Worked with the Germans," "Story of Maximón," "The Legend of Francisco Sojuel: A Tzutuhil Story," and "The Rich and Miserable Man: A Cakchiquel Story."

Stories that have primarily Ladino or European elements include "Simple Simón," "Temperament and the Deeds of the Son of God," "The Grandfather and the Faultfinders," and "The Nuns and the Charcoal Vendor."

Stories that have an obvious mix of Mayan and Ladino cultural characteristics are "Tale of the Teacher," "The Oldest Tale of My Town," "Story of the Señor of Esquipulas," "The Woman Who Died for Three Days and Went to Get Acquainted with Hell," "Story of the Black God, *Dueño* of the Night," "The Fisherman and the King," "The *Sombrerón* and the Blue Fly," and "The Gold and Silver Fish."

As I indicate elsewhere, the tales that Ignacio said he invented are "Story: Everything Was Created," "The Two Brothers and the Fortune," "The Louse Who Caused the Death of the Womanizing King: A Tzutuhil Story," "Story of the Dog and the Cat," and "The Story of the *Tecolote*."

16. Angel Vigil (1994:xxi) notes that proverbs existing alongside folktales is part of the Hispanic tradition in the southwestern United States. My discussion of proverbs in this introduction depends largely on a separate list of Guatemalan proverbs that Ignacio gave me in Spanish, although he did not specifically link the proverbs to the tales.

17. Ignacio called this tale simply "A Tzutuhil Tale." I kept this as the subtitle but added "Heart of Heaven, Heart of Earth" to reflect the main theme of the story.

18. The expression *colorín colorado* is used to signal the end of a folktale of oral or written narration. *Colorado* by itself is used to indicate that a folktale is racy or pornographic.

19. In response to my question about the difference between a *brujo* (witch) and a *characotel* (Sexton 1992a:182), Ignacio explained that the *characotel* is a *nagual* but the

nagual works differently from the *brujo.* The *characotel* is a *nagual* who during the nights converts into an animal such as a cat, a dog, a pig, or an owl. He or she goes to the *sitios* of sick people or to houses to bother people when they are sleeping. If the person is frightened, the *characotel* has an influence, or a hypnotic power, over the person, who falls sick. If the sickness isn't cured by a *zajorín* (shaman), the person dies. A *brujo* has a *nagual* and a power of *el mundo* (*dueño del mundo* [god of the world, earth]). He is able to bewitch a person by doing certain *secretos,* or ritual acts. He takes the bones of the dead out of cemeteries and leaves or buries them in the *sitio* of some enemy. Also, a *brujo* can be contracted by others to bewitch someone.

20. As in the folktales of the *Zinacantecos* (people of Zinacantán) of Chiapas, Mexico, there seems to be a fear of blacks found in the folktales of the Tzutuhil Maya. As Laughlin and Karasik (in Sexton 1992b:242–243) suggest, the reason may be rooted in horrendous stories that the Spanish conquerors told about blacks to prevent the formation of alliances between runaway slaves and the American Indian populations. Also, in some instances, black slaves were treated by the Spanish conquerors as confidants, and they were put in supervisory roles over Indian serfs. In any case, since there are no blacks living in the Lake Atitlán region, the Indians there view them as something of a mystery. Furthermore, this folktale assumes the reader is aware of the belief in *susto,* a phenomenon in which victims can die of fright.

21. As documented in *Son of Tecún Umán* (Sexton 1990), residents of this region were often forced to provide their labor free, a kind of corvée.

22. The military draft has been harsh for young men, especially Indians, who are eighteen years of age or more. It is not unusual for young men to be physically pressed into service by gangs that capture them on the streets and haul them off to basic training camps without notifying their families. The young men are conscripted for a period of thirty months (Sexton 1990; Keefe 1983).

23. Ignacio says he invented this tale himself. Nevertheless, it has a number of interesting elements. In the previous tales, Heart of Heaven and Heart of Earth are treated as separate gods, but the present tale raises the question of whether Heart of Heaven is a primordial deity that embodies both masculine and feminine characteristics. While Ignacio insists that *Corazón del cielo, Corazón de la tierra* (Heart of Heaven, Heart of Earth) are separate gods, he says that *Corazón de la tierra* is also called *el dueño del mundo,* or *santo mundo,* and that while these terms are similar, they are not exactly the same. He continues to say that *Corazón de la tierra* is also referred to as *madre tierra,* or Mother Earth. Ignacio notes, however, that *madre tierra* is not a separate goddess, just a respectful way of referring to *santo mundo.* He cautions that one does not say *la dueña del santo mundo,* rather *el dueño del santo mundo.* Ignacio says, "The phrase *la madre tierra* is used because that is where we fathers eat, where we plant, where we work. When one is small, the mother gives one everything; she gives food, everything, and for that reason we call it *madre tierra.*" Ignacio speculates that some individuals see the earth deity as having masculine characteristics while others view it as having feminine traits. He says this is similar to the way the deity of Lake Atitlán is viewed by some as masculine and by others as feminine, depending on the person.

Tedlock (1983:271) points out that dualities in the thought of the Quichés and other Indians of Mesoamerica are complementary, not oppositional, and contemporaneous, not sequential. Henry Nicholson (1971:410–411, 420–422) discusses the sexual duality concept in the Ometeotl complex of deities for pre-Hispanic Central Mexico and the Earth-

Mother concept in the Teteoinnan complex. Thompson (1971:196) considers a similar phenomenon for the classic Maya by pointing out that the sky (heaven) is considered male and the earth female and that their intercourse is thought to mystically bring life to the world. Nathaniel Tarn and Martin Prechtel (1986:173) state that the Tzutuhiles of Santiago Atitlán conceive "male and female aspects of one original unit and [believe] that no unit can be other than male female." One example they give comes from the anatomy of human female and male sexual organs: the clitoris is considered male and the urethra of the penis is thought to be a small vagina.

In a similar vein, Wilson (1995:66–67) speaks of the sexual dualism of the mountain spirits for the Q'eqchi' of Guatemala. He states that the female earth does not have a separate name, such as the Andean Pachamama (Mother Earth). "The Q'eqchi' landscape can be both female and male at the same time, even if a tzuultaq'a (mountain spirit) is male. The mountain spirit is called 'Our Father Our Mother,' regardless of its sex. The sex of the land is thus contextual."

Ignacio explicitly states that Heart of Heaven, Heart of Earth are deities with mysterious powers. Michael Singer (1993:11) makes the same point for a similar conception among the Vietnamese: "Father Heaven, Ong Troi, was keeper of all human fate, the master of unseen powers and mysteries. Mother Earth, Me Dat, provided food and water for the wells and fields." The concept of Mother Earth, or Earth-Mother, is widespread throughout the world, especially among agrarian societies of the Americas (Leach and Fried 1984).

24. The old man died on the boca costa, where it is only partly level, because the horse didn't get enough grass. This story explains the existence of the level costa (la costa), the semimountainous region (lower and upper boca costa), and the highlands of Quezaltenango and Santa Cruz del Quiché (los altos), as described in West and Augelli (1989:388–389).

25. Zea is about 88 years old, and he was born in the aldea of Patzilín, San José, but his parents were Quiché.

26. In Tzutuhil, utz means "good" or "it is good" and tii means "meat" or "flesh."

27. Quique didn't tell Ignacio what kind of secretos he had to do, only that he had to do them.

28. In Son of Tecún Umán there is an account of how the Joseños sold their land to the Martineros during the mandamientos (forced labor sponsored by the national government) of the early 1900s that required them to migrate to work on the coastal plantations. The ill-conceived rationale for the forced labor migrations was the promotion of the country's economic growth.

29. The Black Christ is actually in a church in Esquipulas. It is a famous shrine for pilgrims from all over Central and South America. Ignacio explained that the meaning in the folktale (even though it varies from reality) is that the Spaniards believed that the Indians would not worship a light-complected image because they couldn't identify with a saint that didn't have a complexion like their own. So they painted the image brown, but in time it turned black from the smoke of the incense and dirt that collected in the church. According to most of the literature, Quiro Cataño, a colonial sculptor, made the human-size image from balsam so that it would be dark. Over the ages, dirt and smoke from incense and candles have turned it shiny black. There is speculation that in the church where the image is kept there is also a hidden, pre-Colombian image that the Indians worshiped earlier (Sapia Martino 1964; Dombrowski 1970; Moore 1973).

30. When I asked Ignacio to explain this, he stated that the couple had told the people that they were going to make the pilgrimage. They were so poor, however, that they couldn't make the trip. The spirit of the image of the Black Christ knew that they had promised to go but didn't. Therefore, the Black Christ punished the couple for deceiving him and the townspeople. In other words, *Vuestro sí, sea sí, and vuestro no, no* (Let your yes mean yes and your no mean no, or do what you say you're going to do).

31. The people do not usually refer to the image as the *Cristo Negro* because they feel that is offensive. Instead, they call it *El Señor de Esquipulas,* which really means "the Black Christ of Esquipulas."

32. Ignacio added as a point of clarification that if you do not respect the saints, you will be punished like Pascual and Catarina. Before you say you are going to do something, think about whether you actually can before you commit yourself to saying you intend to do so, because if you can't follow through with what you say you are going to do, you may suffer the consequences.

33. Elena Bizarro and Bonifacio Soto are Ignacio's blood mother and her blood brother (Ignacio's uncle on his mother's side).

34. Elena de Dios is the woman living *juntos* (joined, or as a common-law spouse) with Ramón Antonio, Ignacio's son. They are living together in a separate house on Ignacio's *sitio*. She is a Quiché whose grandparents were from Totonicapán. She was born in an *aldea* (village) of San José la Laguna.

35. Many Tzutuhil people think the owl and the cat have equal power to do bad things.

36. At the end of this story, Ignacio wrote, "The truth is, this story is an arrangement [invention] of a Tzutuhil *Joseño* [Ignacio] who lives by working in the field as always a campesino, but also in his free time he is dedicated to writing stories and other things."

37. Another tale whose content is about a similar enchanted hill in another place, in which people have to pay for their wealth in this life with their souls in the next life, appears in *Mayan Folktales* (Sexton 1992b) under the title "Story of the Enchanted Hill, Tun Abaj."

38. In response to my query, Ignacio explained that this was a way of controlling the number of animals that persons could hunt with permission of *el mundo* (*dueño del mundo,* lord of the earth). Some people hunt without permission, and they do not have the protection of the *dueño*.

39. In Tzutuhil, *Camibal* means "where one dies" or "where there is death."

40. Ignacio added that his Uncle Gerardo Bizarro Ramos, now deceased, told him this story mainly because Gerardo was a hunter and Ignacio went with him when he was a young boy. Also, Ignacio said that his uncle Bonifacio Soto, son of his grandmother Isabel, was not a hunter but heard the tale from his family members. Martín Coj, Ignacio's adoptive father, and Clemente Coché Pantzay, the grandfather of Ignacio's wife, Anica, were both hunters. Ignacio and his kin once killed two deer in San José and two in San Benito la Laguna. Ignacio saw that four times they carried the bones to the Paruchi Abaj Hill. It took only twenty to twenty-five minutes to arrive at the hill from San José la Laguna. Regarding this ritual, Ignacio said, "If one person kills the deer, he has to go. If two people kill the deer, they have to go take the bones. If three people kill the deer, all three have to take the bones and perform the *costumbre*. But the *costumbre* with the bones is different from the *costumbre* asking for permission to hunt in the first place. In the *costumbre* with the bones, there are incense, candles, [and] rum, [but] not meat."

Ignacio said that there are many old people in his town who know this popular tale. His grandmother Isabel knew it too.

41. Valeriano Temó told this story to Ramón Antonio, Ignacio's son, who in turn told Ignacio. Valeriano Temó is a native *Joseño* who now lives in Guatemala City and who works for INDE (Institucional Nacional de Electrificación). In *Son of Tecún Umán,* Ignacio documents the arrival of electricity in San José in July of 1974. He recalls that people were afraid to leave their houses at night because they thought the electric generators in Santa María Quezaltenango needed human bodies to produce electrical energy. Some people thought that Ignacio and a friend, Diego José Ramos Rodríguez, had an obligation to turn over to the jefe of the electric institute a certain number of people as food for light. Everyone was afraid of Ignacio, and people were saying bad things about him. He had to go to court to stop the rumors. After the people of San José became accustomed to having electric lights in the streets, they soon forgot about their fears. Ignacio says, however, that some people still believe that electricity requires human heads. When they see the transformers, they ask if they have heads.

42. Ignacio said he invented this story. For another story that deals with the creation of animals, see "The Two Real Children of God: There Were Only Two, Grandfather and Grandmother" in *Mayan Folktales* (Sexton 1992b).

43. In *Campesino* (Sexton 1985:251) Ignacio recorded an episode about having three sick children. He was so worried that he did not sleep the entire night, partly because at 2:00 A.M. two owls, an omen of death, arrived and made noise above his house.

44. This statement about giving away a pony is just a way of ending a story if the storyteller has an audience such as children.

45. As Norman Schwartz (1983:152) points out, Maximón (also known as Saint Simón, Hermano [Brother] Simón, Judas Iscariot, and Don Pedro de Alvarado) is a widespread figure in the popular religion of contemporary Guatemala, including the Petén region and Chimaltenango. The *cofradías* of Maximón are not authorized by the Catholic Church, primarily because petitioners may ask for financial or sexual favors or even request that an enemy be bewitched, all requests that a person would not ask from the other saints (Tax and Hinshaw 1969; Schwartz 1983). Jody Glittenberg (1994:165), who writes about a shrine at San Andrés Itzapa, says that her informants told her it was "the sinful nature of Maximón that attracts fellow transgressors—those who lie and cheat, drink booze, and who want wealth, good luck, and good health." Thus, Maximón represents the sinners of the world.

As Orellana (1975:847, 1981) and Dennis Tedlock (1997:221) note, Maximón is a syncretic blend of Mayan and Christian figures such as the old Mayan god Mam and the Christian Saint Simón. Belief in Maximón is of uncertain origin, but it seems to have emerged in the nineteenth century (Tax and Hinshaw 1969; Schwartz 1983; Glittenberg 1994). The most famous Maximón resides in Santiago Atitlán. From there his following spread with separate images to other lakeside towns such as Panajachel and San José.

Robert Carlsen (1997:172-173) believes that scholars have mistranslated the name Maximón. Rather than being a composite of Mam and Simón, Carlsen argues that *Maximón* means "Mr. Knotted" (in reference to how he was constructed), since in Tzutuhil *ma* means "mister" and *xim* means "knot."

The image of Maximón is thought to have the human attributes of being able to drink *aguardiente* and smoke tobacco. In the Mam language, *max* means "tobacco," and the image of Maximón usually appears with a cigar between his lips (Sexton 1990:15).

In San José ordinary members of the Catholic Church equate Maximón with the devil, and they do not have much respect for him. According to Ignacio Bizarro Ujpán, however, the shamans are so respectful of Maximón that they address him only as Don Pedro de Alvarado, whom they consider a saint because he was valiant and conquered Guatemala. More or less, he is another god to them (Sexton 1990:160–161).

For a Tzutuhil tale from Santiago Atitlán about a holy man, or *Nagual Achá,* who is believed to make miracles and who summons the help of Maximón, see "The Black Man and the Volcano" in Orellana (1975:863–865).

46. The idea here is that the *zajorines* transformed themselves into their spiritual forms and went across the lake.

47. In Sexton and Bizarro (n.d.) Ignacio documents the killings that took place in Santiago Atitlán, including the massacre in December of 1990 in which thirteen Tzutuhiles were killed by an army unit bivouacked in a coffee grove near the town. In December of 1996, as final peace negotiations were being worked out between the guerrillas and the army, questions were raised as to whether those who committed wartime atrocities should be granted amnesty (Cormier 1996:10).

48. In dedicating their performance on the cassette to Francisco Sojuel, the musicians used his name in Tzutuhil, which is Apalas Sojuel. In this tale Ignacio uses the Tzutuhil term *ajtzujila* to refer to the group, and he provides the Spanish translation *(flor de maíz)* in parentheses. The affix *aj* in Tzutuhil is used to derive nouns (Dayley 1984:174), and the word *aj* means *elote* (ear of green corn) in Tzutuhil (Dayley 1984:143) and in Cakchiquel (Rodríguez Guaján et al. 1990:144). Also, Jorge Arriola (1973:636) indicates that the word *Tzutuhil* itself means *flor de maíz* (flower of corn), since *tzutuj* means flower and *jil,* an alteration of *jal* in Cakchiquel, means *mazorca* (ear or cob of corn). According to Carlsen (1997:41), there was a regional preconquest polity to which the name Tzutuhil refers, and a literal translation of Tzutuhil is "Flower of the Maize Plant."

49. Teodoro is a *principal* and native of Santiago Atitlán, more or less some 70 years of age, who still holds an office in the Catholic Church.

50. Of course, elephants exist only in zoos in the New World, but this is a story that Ignacio invented, and it should be classified as a contemporary tale.

51. Daniel Armas (1991:197) describes the *sombrerón* as a personality of popular myth, represented by an individual of small stature who, carrying a big sombrero that covers his face, is able to charm the travelers that he surprises on the road in the night. Two other stories about the *sombrerón,* both different from Ignacio's version, appear in Francisco Barnoya (1974) and Luis Arango (1984).

52. Ignacio titled this tale "Our Bread." I changed the title to reflect more of the content of the tale. Anthony Campos (1977:55–57) provides a shorter but similar tale from Mexico with the same theme of harvesting what you sow. In both tales, farmers with positive attitudes have abundant harvests while those with negative attitudes sow rocks.

53. For another folktale dealing with individuals with supernatural ability to make rain, see "The Story of the *Poder* [Power, Ability] of Persons When They Are Born" in *Mayan Folktales* (Sexton 1992b:52–58).

54. This tale illustrates a Confucian sense of filial piety in that it reinforces the idea that children should always obey their parents, even when the parents' demands are outlandish.

Glossary

aguardiente—cane liquor

ajkum(es)—shaman(s)

alcalde—head, mayor

aldea(s)—village(s)

alguacil(es)—runner(s), aide(s), especially in a *cofradía*

aniz—anise

Atiteca(s), Atiteco(s)—woman (women), man (men), person (people) of Santiago Atitlán; see also *Santiagueña(s), Santiagueño(s)*

atol—ritual corn drink

ayote(s)—gourd(s), pumpkin(s)

bajareque—cane and mud

bartolina—small and dark prison cell

bejucal—patch of lianas

Beniteña(s), Beniteño(s)—woman (women), man (men), person (people) of San Benito

blancos—whites

bravo—angry, strong, mean

brujo(s)—witch(es)

Buenos días—Good morning

caites—open-toed sandals

camineros—roadmen

camote(s)—sweet potato(es)

cangrejeros—crab fishermen

cantiles—very poisonous snakes of hot climates *(agkistrodon bilineatus)*

cantones—barrios

chan—herb whose seeds are small black grains

characotel(es)—person (people) who can turn into a *nagual(es)*, or animal form(s)

of a person (people) or spirit(s), and act as a spy (spies) or do evil; person (people) similar to a witch(es)

chicha—corn liquor

chichicaste—nettle

chilacayote(s)—large gourd(s) fed to cattle

chirimía—wind instrument similar to an oboe

cielo—heaven, sky

cofrades—members of a *cofradía*

cofradía—religious brotherhood

colorado—racy or obscene

colorín colorado—expression to indicate the end of a story or some written or spoken narration

comadre—co-mother, godmother, friend

compadres—co-parents, godparents, friends

corazón—heart, center

costumbre(s)—ritual(s), custom(s)

culo—ass, anus

culote—see *culo*

cusha—*chicha*, corn liquor, home brew

dueña(s), dueño(s)—owner(s), lord(s), master(s), goddess(es), god(s)

dueño del (santo) mundo—god of the (sacred) world, earth

el mundo—see *dueño del (santo) mundo*

elote—ear of green corn

faja—cloth belt or sash

finca—farm, plantation

flor de maíz—flower of corn

gracias—thanks

guaro—firewater, sugarcane rum

güisquil(es)—chayote(s) *(Scehium edule)*,

whose fruit is the size of an orange
and whose fruit, root, and flowers are
edible (and eaten)

habladas—words being said, speech

hombres de maíz—men of corn

huevos—eggs, testicles

indígenas—Indians, indigenes

invierno—winter, rainy season

itz'el tak' winak—demons, the Spaniards

jocotal—tree or plantation of *jocotes*

jocote—hog plum

Joseña(s), Joseño(s)—woman (women), man
(men), person (people) of San José

Juanera(s), Juanero(s)—woman (women),
man (men), person (people) of San Juan

juntos—joined, common-law marriage

lengua—native tongue, language

maestro—teacher

mandamientos—forced labor sponsored by
the national government

Marqueña(s), Marqueño(s)—woman
(women), man (men), person (people)
of San Marcos

Martinera(s), Martinero(s)—woman
(women), man (men), person (people)
of San Martín

masa—corn dough

mashtate—loincloth

mazorca—ear or cob of corn

mojón—landmark

morenos—blacks who are speakers of
Carib

muchá—muchachos, boys

municipio—municipal district, town

nagual—person's spiritual or animal form

Nahualeña(s), Nahualeño(s)—woman
(women), man (men), person (people)
of Nahualá

nataá, nuteé, watit, numamaá—fathers, mothers,
grandfathers, grandmothers

naturales—natives, Indians

negros—blacks

ocote—resinous pine

panteón—above-ground tomb

Pedrana(s), Pedrano(s)—woman (women),
man (men), person (people) of San Pedro

petates—palm mats

piedra de moler—arm of the grinding stone

pipe—male member, penis

pita(s)—fiber(s) made from the agave plant

polaco—cop

principal—town elder

quintales—measures of weight of 100
pounds each

rancho, ranchito—cane hut or small, rustic
house

real(es)—former monetary unit and coin
of Spain and its possessions, money

rubios—blonds

Ruc'ux Caj, Ruc'ux Uleep—Heart of
Heaven, Heart of Earth

Sanjoseños—see *Joseña(s), Joseño(s)*

Santiagueña(s), Santiagueño(s)—woman
(women), man (men), person (people)
of Santiago Atitlán

secreto—magical or sacred rite or object

sitio—homesite, land

Sololateca(s), Sololateco(s)—woman
(women), man (men), person (people)
of Sololá

sombrerón—personality of popular myth,
represented by an individual of small
stature who, carrying a big sombrero
that covers his face, is able to charm
the travelers that he surprises on the
road in the night

suerte—luck, fate

susto—fright, psychological illness

taltuza(s)—rodent(s) that carve(s) long tunnels
in the earth

tarjeta de vialidad—*libreto*, card (passport)
proving one was not a vagabond

tecolote—owl

tecomate—gourd or gourd jar

temascal—sweat house

tepescuinte—brown rodent with black
stripes on its back

tercio—portion of firewood a man can
carry on his back

texel—low-ranking office in a *cofradía*
held by a woman

tierra—earth, land

tinaco—large, thick, clay vat of water

tonal—companion animal or destiny

totopostes—tortillas of coarsely ground and toasted corn

tragos—drinks, shots

traje de bailador—dancer's suit

vialidad—see *tarjeta de vialidad*

viaje—ceremony, trip

viejito(s)—old man (men), old people, old folks, elders

zajorín—shaman

Zinacanteca(s), Zinacanteco(s)—woman (women), man (men), person (people) of Zinacantán

References Cited

Adams, Richard, and Arthur Rubel
    1969   Sickness and Social Relations. In *Handbook of Middle American Indians,*
            vol. 6, *Social Anthropology,* edited by Manning Nash, pp. 333–356. Austin:
            University of Texas Press.
Andrade, Manuel J.
    1946   *Materials on the Quiché, Cakchiquel, and Tzutujil Languages.* Microfilm
            Collection of Manuscripts on Cultural Anthropology, No. 11, The Joseph
            Regenstein Library, The University of Chicago.
Arango, Luis Alfredo
    1984   *Las lágrimas del Sombrerón.* Guatemala City: Editorial Piedra Santa,
            Colección Colorín Colorado.
Armas, Daniel
    1991   *Diccionario de la Expresión Popular Guatemalteca.* Guatemala City: Editorial
            Piedra Santa.
Arriola, Jorge Luis
    1973   *El Libro de las Geonimias de Guatemala: Diccionario Etimólogico.* Guatemala
            City: Seminario de Integración Social Guatemalteca.
Barnoya Gálvez, Francisco
    1974   *Cuentos y Leyendas de Guatemala.* Guatemala City: Editorial Piedra Santa.
Berdan, Frances
    1982   *The Aztecs of Central Mexico: An Imperial Society.* New York: Holt, Rinehart,
            and Winston.
Birdsell, Joseph B.
    1951   The Problem of the Early Peopling of the Americas as Viewed from Asia.
            In *Papers on the Physical Anthropology of the American Indian,* pp. 1–38. New
            York: The Viking Fund, Inc.
    1972   *Human Evolution: An Introduction to the New Physical Anthropology.* Chicago:
            Rand McNally & Company.
Boyd, Robert S.
    1998   New Data Backdates New World Arrivals. *The Arizona Republic,* 17 Febru-
            ary, p. A3.

Campos, Anthony John
1977   *Mexican Folktales.* Tucson: The University of Arizona Press.
Cancian, Frank
1965   *Economics and Prestige in a Mayan Community.* Palo Alto: Stanford University Press.
Carlsen, Robert S.
1997   *The War for the Heart and Soul of a Highland Maya Town.* Austin: University of Texas Press.
Carlsen, Robert S., and Martin Prechtel
1991   The Flowering of the Dead: An Interpretation of Highland Maya Culture. *Man* 26(1):23–42.
Carmack, Robert
1981   *The Quiché Mayas of Utatlán: The Evolution of a Guatemalan Kingdom.* Norman: University of Oklahoma Press.
Carmack, Robert, et al.
1997   Introduction. In *The Legacy of Mesoamerica: History and Culture of a Native American Civilization,* edited by Robert Carmack et al., pp. 1–38. New Jersey: Prentice Hall.
Castaneda, Carlos
1968   *The Teachings of Don Juan: A Yaqui Way of Knowledge.* Berkeley and Los Angeles: University of California Press.
1971   *A Separate Reality: Further Conversations with Don Juan.* New York: Simon and Schuster.
1972   *Journey to Ixtlán: The Lessons of Don Juan.* New York: Simon and Schuster.
1974   *Tales of Power.* New York: Simon and Schuster.
Christopher, Renny
1995   *The Viet Nam War/The American War: Images and Representations in Euro-American and Vietnamese Exile Narratives.* Amherst: University of Massachusetts Press.
Cojtí Cuxil, Demetrio
1996   The Politics of Maya Revindication. In *Maya Cultural Activism in Guatemala,* edited by Edward F. Fischer and R. McKenna Brown, pp. 19–50. Austin: University of Texas Press.
Colby, Benjamin, and Lore M. Colby
1981   *The Daykeeper: The Life and Discourse of an Ixil Diviner.* Cambridge: Harvard University Press.
Cormier, Bill
1996   Guatemalan Wartime Atrocities Raise Questions over Amnesty. *Arizona Daily Sun,* 3 December, p. 10.
Dayley, Jon P.
1985   *Tzutujil Grammar.* Vol. 7, University of California Publications, Linguistics. Berkeley and Los Angeles: University of California Press.
de Paz, Marco, and Marcus de Paz
1991   *Calendario Maya: El Camino Infinito del Tiempo.* Guatemala City: Ediciones Gran Jaguar.

Dombroski, John, et al.
1970   *Area Handbook for Guatemala.* Washington, D.C.: U.S. Government Printing Office.
England, Nora
1996   The Role of Language Standardization in Revitalization. In *Maya Cultural Activism in Guatemala,* edited by Edward F. Fischer and R. McKenna Brown, pp. 178–194. Austin: University of Texas Press.
England, Nora, et al.
1993   *Maya' Chil': Los Idiomas Mayas de Guatemala.* Guatemala City: Editorial Cholsamaj.
Fischer, Edward F., and R. McKenna Brown (editors)
1996   Introduction. In *Maya Cultural Activism in Guatemala,* edited by Edward F. Fischer and R. McKenna Brown, pp. 1–18. Austin: University of Texas Press.
Fleming, Ilah
1966   Carib. In *Languages of Guatemala,* edited by Marvin K. Mayers, Summer Institute of Linguistics, pp. 303–308. The Hague: Mouton and Company.
Foster, George
1968   "Comment" in the discussion of Charles Wisdom's "The Supernatural World and Curing." In *Heritage of Conquest,* by Sol Tax et al., pp. 134–141. New York: Cooper Square Publishers, Inc. (1st ed. The Macmillan Company 1952)
Frazer, Sir James George
1963   *The Golden Bough.* Abridged ed. New York: Collier Books.
Glittenberg, Jody
1994   *To the Mountain and Back: The Mysteries of Guatemalan Highland Family Life.* Prospect Heights, Illinois: Waveland Press.
Goetz, Delia (translator)
1953   *Title of the Lords of Totonicapán.* Norman: University of Oklahoma Press.
Goetz, Delia, Sylvanus G. Morley, and Adrián Recinos
1950   *Popol Vuh: The Sacred Book of the Ancient Quiché Maya.* Norman: University of Oklahoma Press.
Hayslip, Le Ly, and Jay Wurts
1989   *When Heaven and Earth Changed Places.* New York: Doubleday.
Herbruger, Alfredo Jr., and Eduardo Díaz Barrios
1956   *Método Para Aprender a Hablar, Leer, y Escribir la Lengua Cakchiquel, Tomo Uno.* Guatemala: Tipografía Nacional.
Justeson, John S., and George A. Broadwell
1997   Language and Languages in Mesoamerica. In *The Legacy of Mesoamerica: History and Culture of a Native American Civilization,* edited by Robert M. Carmack et al., pp. 379–406. New Jersey: Prentice Hall.
Kaufman, Terrence
1974   *Idiomas de Mesoamérica.* Guatemala City: Editorial José de Pineda Ibarra.
Keefe, Eugene K.
1983   National Security. In *Guatemala: A Country Study,* edited by Richard F. Nyrop, pp. 177–218. Washington, D.C.: U.S. Government Printing Office.

Kluck, P. A.

1983   The Society and Its Environment. In *Guatemala: A Country Study*, edited by Richard F. Nyrop, pp. 41–82. Washington, D.C.: U.S. Government Printing Office.

Laughlin, Robert M., and Carol Karasik

1988   *The People of the Bat: Mayan Tales and Dreams from Zinacantán.* Washington, D.C.: Smithsonian Institution Press.

Leach, Maria, and Jerome Fried

1984   *Funk & Wagnalls Standard Dictionary of Folklore, Mythology, and Legend.* San Francisco: HarperSanFrancisco.

McKinley, Jesse

1996   "Ebonics" Stirs National Debate: Is It a Dialect, Language, or Sham? *The Arizona Republic,* 22 December, p. A31.

Moore, Richard E.

1973   *Historical Dictionary of Guatemala.* Revised ed. Metuchen, New Jersey: The Scarecrow Press, Inc.

Nicholson, Henry B.

1971   Religion in Pre-Hispanic Central Mexico. In *Handbook of Middle American Indians, Archeology of Northern Mesoamerica, Part One,* vol. 10, edited by Gordon F. Ekholm and Ignacio Bernal, pp. 395–446. Austin: University of Texas Press.

Orellana, Sandra L.

1975   Folk Literature of the Tzutujil Maya. *Anthropos* 70:840–876.

1981   Idols and Idolatry in Highland Guatemala. *Ethnohistory* 28:157–177.

1987   *Indian Medicine in Highland Guatemala: The Pre-Hispanic and Colonial Periods.* Albuquerque: University of New Mexico Press.

Perera, Victor

1993   *Unfinished Conquest: The Guatemalan Tragedy.* Berkeley and Los Angeles: University of California Press.

Piedra Santa A., Julio

1994   *Geografía Visualizada.* 13th printing. Guatemala City: Editorial Piedra Santa.

Rodríguez Guaján, Demetrio, et al.

1990   *Ch'uticholtzij Maya-Kaqchikel.* Guatemala: Editorial Kamar.

Saler, Benson

1964   Nagual, Witch, and Sorcerer in a Quiché Village. *Ethnology* 3(3):305–328.

Sapia Martino, Raúl

1964   *Guatemala: Mayaland of Eternal Spring.* Buenos Aires: River Plato Publishing Company.

Saravia E., Albertina

1980   *Popol Wuh: Ancient Stories of the Quiche Indians of Guatemala.* Guatemala City: Editorial Piedra Santa.

Schwartz, Norman

1983   San Simón: Ambiguity and Identity in Petén, Guatemala. *Sociologus* 33(2):152–173.

Sexton, James D.

1972   *Education and Innovation in a Guatemalan Community: San Juan la Laguna.* Latin

American Studies Series, vol. 19. Los Angeles: University of California, Los Angeles.

1978   Protestantism and Modernization in Two Guatemalan Towns. *American Ethnologist* 5:280–302.

1979a   Modernization among Cakchiquel Maya: An Analysis of Responses to Line Drawings. *Journal of Cross-Cultural Psychology* 10:173–190.

1979b   Education and Acculturation in Highland Guatemala. *Anthropology and Education Quarterly* 10:80–95.

Sexton, James D. (translator and editor)

1985   *Campesino: The Diary of a Guatemalan Indian.* Tucson: The University of Arizona Press.

1990   *Son of Tecún Umán: A Maya Indian Tells His Life History.* Prospect Heights, Illinois: Waveland Press. (1st ed. The University of Arizona Press 1981)

1992a   *Ignacio: The Diary of a Maya Indian of Guatemala.* Philadelphia: University of Pennsylvania Press.

1992b   *Mayan Folktales: Folklore from Lake Atitlán, Guatemala.* New York: Doubleday Anchor.

Sexton, James D., and Ignacio Bizarro Ujpán

n.d.   Ms. tentatively titled *Joseño: The Diary of a Maya Indian of Guatemala.*

Sexton, James D., and Clyde M. Woods

n.d.   Ms. tentatively titled *Field Notes from Fifteen Guatemalan Towns, Lake Atitlán (1968–1975).*

1977   Development and Modernization among Highland Maya: A Comparative Analysis of Ten Guatemalan Towns. *Human Organization* 36:156–177.

1982   Demography, Development and Modernization in Fourteen Highland Guatemalan Towns. In *The Historical Demography of Highland Guatemala,* edited by Robert M. Carmack, John Early, and Christopher Lutz. Institute for Mesoamerican Studies, SUNY at Albany, Pub. No. 6, pp. 189–202. Austin: University of Texas Press.

Sharon, Douglas

1978   *Wizard of the Four Winds: A Shaman's Story.* New York: The Free Press.

Singer, Michael

1993   The Story. In *The Making of Oliver Stone's* Heaven and Earth, pp. 12–102. Boston: Charles E. Tuttle Company, Inc.

Tarn, Nathaniel, and Martin Prechtel

1986   Constant Inconstancy: The Feminine Principle in Atiteco Mythology. In *Symbol and Meaning beyond the Closed Community: Essays in Mesoamerican Ideas,* edited by Gary H. Gossen, pp. 173–184. Albany: Institute for Mesoamerican Studies.

Tax, Sol

1946   *The Towns of Lake Atitlán.* Microfilm Collection of Manuscripts on Middle American Cultural Anthropology, No. 13, The Joseph Regenstein Library, The University of Chicago.

1968   Descripción Sumaria de los Pueblos. In *Los Pueblos del Lago de Atitlán,* by Sol Tax et al., pp. 17–40. Guatemala: Seminario de Integración Social Guatemalteca.

Tax, Sol, and Robert Hinshaw
    1969   The Maya of the Midwestern Highlands. In *Handbook of Middle American Indians: Ethnology, Part I,* edited by Evon Z. Vogt, pp. 69–100. Austin: University of Texas Press.

Tedlock, Barbara
    1992   *Time and the Highland Maya.* Revised ed. Albuquerque: University of New Mexico Press.

Tedlock, Dennis
    1983   *The Spoken Word and the Work of Interpretation.* Philadelphia: University of Pennsylvania Press.
    1985   *Popol Vuh: The Definitive Edition of the Mayan Book of the Dawn of Life and the Glories of Gods and Kings.* New York: Simon and Schuster.
    1996   *Popol Vuh: The Definitive Edition of the Mayan Book of the Dawn of Life and the Glories of Gods and Kings.* Revised ed. New York: Simon and Schuster.
    1997   *Breath on the Mirror: Mythic Voices and Visions of the Living Maya.* Albuquerque: University of New Mexico Press.

Terada, Alice M.
    1989   *Under the Starfruit Tree.* Honolulu: University of Hawaii Press.

Thompson, J. Eric S.
    1970   *Maya History and Religion.* Norman: University of Oklahoma Press.
    1971   *Maya Hieroglyphic Writing.* Norman: University of Oklahoma Press.

Vigil, Angel
    1994   *The Corn Woman: Stories and Legends of the Hispanic Southwest.* Englewood, Colorado: Libraries Unlimited, Inc.

Warren, Kay
    1989   *The Symbolism of Subordination: Indian Identity in a Guatemalan Town.* 2nd ed. Austin: University of Texas Press.

West, Robert C., and John P. Augelli
    1966   *Middle America: Its Lands and Peoples.* Englewood Cliffs: Prentice-Hall, Inc.
    1989   *Middle America: Its Lands and Peoples.* 3rd ed. Englewood Cliffs: Prentice-Hall, Inc.

Wilson, Richard
    1995   *Maya Resurgence in Guatemala: Q'eqchi' Experiences.* Norman: University of Oklahoma Press.

Wisdom, Charles
    1968   The Supernatural World and Curing. In *Heritage of Conquest,* by Sol Tax et al., pp. 119–134. New York: Cooper Square Publishers, Inc. (1st ed. The Macmillan Company 1952)

Woods, Clyde M.
    1975   *Culture Change.* Dubuque, Iowa: Wm. C. Brown.

Wright, Ronald
    1991   *Time among the Maya.* New York: Henry Holt and Company.

About the Authors

James D. Sexton has been working in Guatemala for the past twenty-eight years. In addition to *Education and Innovation in a Guatemalan Community,* he has written a number of articles on modernization and cultural change in highland Guatemala. Since receiving a Ph.D. in cultural anthropology from UCLA in 1973, Sexton has been teaching at Northern Arizona University, where in 1982 he received the NAU President's Award for excellence in teaching, research, and service. In 1991 he was named Regents' Professor, and in 1997 he was selected as the NAU Phi Kappa Phi Faculty Scholar. A past president of the Southwestern Anthropological Association, Sexton has traveled extensively throughout Mexico, Central America, South America, and the Caribbean. He and his wife, a medical social worker, have one son, Randy, a student at the University of Arizona.

Ignacio Bizarro Ujpán is a *principal,* or town elder, of San José la Laguna. He has served in a number of civil and religious offices in his town. His religious service includes a year as the *alcalde* (head) of the *cofradías* (religious brotherhoods) of María Concepción and of San Juan Bautista, the two most important *cofradías* of his town. His civil service includes a term as *síndico,* or town syndic, the second-highest elected office. He writes in his spare time, when he is away from his cornfields and coffee groves and when he is not helping his wife, a Tzutuhil Maya Indian, with her weaving projects. They have nine children and three grandchildren. Their eldest daughter and younger son are among the few Indian students of San José who have attained their teaching credentials.